The Volley Girls' Book of Life, Love, and Unforced Errors

By

Karen C. Rasberry

ISBN: 1-4140-1497-X (e-book)
ISBN: 1-4140-1498-8 (Paperback)

Library of Congress Control Number: 2003098536

This book is printed on acid free paper.

Printed in the United States of America
Bloomington, IN

1stBooks - rev. 11/24/03

Contents

To
my daughter...my joy, the most
creative and unique person I have
ever known,
and to my son...my pride, who possesses
more character and grit than
he ever imagined,
and to my faithful husband...the fisherman,
who inadvertently forced me
into a life of tennis,
and to the Volley Girls...my friends,
who have enriched my life with their
diversity, wit, and wisdom.

Introduction

Numerous "everything-you-ever-wanted-to-know" books have been written about the game of tennis. Many of those books focus on the progression of the game into a professional sport and the players who made their mark on the court. Obviously, a great percentage of the people who play tennis never achieve professional status. If it were easy, we would have all done it ourselves. Likewise, that tiny fraction of players who do become professionals never find themselves in Center Court at Wimbledon or the winner of the elusive Grand Slam.

Since I am merely a tennis-playing nobody and have no bona fide credentials (literary or athletic) to speak of, this book is not intended to be an in-depth history of the sport, nor is it a guide to improving your game. You can read about how to improve your serve or your forehand or what to do when you are down five points in a tiebreak elsewhere. Reading about how to improve your game is grand, but genuine improvement comes only when you can apply what you have read in a real live match when the pressure is on, your hands are shaking, your stomach is churning, and your heart is about to beat out of your chest. It all seems so simple on paper, but is often impossible to execute when the chips are down.

It is because I am one of the hundreds of thousands of nobodies who is hopelessly addicted to tennis that I have written this book.

They (who are "they"?) say that every person on this planet who is literate and still registers brain waves on an EEG has more than enough material stored in his gray matter to write at least one book. As it took me seven days to write the first six words, I had serious doubts about that myth. It was quite a stretch to get these scattered and confused brain cells of mine to stick together long enough to summon up a book. My brain, which was wired nearly a half century ago, is prone to short circuit. In my thirties, my train of thought could be held for at least sixty seconds. Currently, as my odometer is clicking toward fifty at frightening speed, I find that my brain can be derailed by the slightest blip on the computer screen.

Several months ago, after tossing and turning half the night, the bizarre idea to write a mostly humorous, sometimes serious, book about women who play tennis, hit me right between the eyes like a forehand volley.

"Nah, that's ridiculous," my somber inner self argued.

So, I just shrugged it off and chalked up my far-fetched idea to another mid-life crisis or a hormone fluctuation. The next night, (to quote Yogi Berra) "it was deja-vu all over again." After a solid week of sleepless nights, my idealist inner self had not relented. Something had to give.

At 2:02 a.m., on that final bug-eyed night, the part of me that never really sleeps, demanded, "Get up right now you spineless procrastinator and put one sentence into the computer."

"O.K., all right!! My Lord. I'll write just one dadburn sentence if you will shut up and let me get some sleep."

My tennis game was presently in a disturbing slump, critical but stable, with no cure in sight. My partner and I had most recently succumbed to a team whose combined ages were 145. Appropriately, and in reference to those players who always seem to take you by surprise, my very first sentence was, "They will beat you every time." After that first sentence I would like to be able to boast that the rest of the words flowed from my brain to my fingertips as prolifically and masterfully as Stephen King's. They absolutely did not. On some days the words came as easily and relaxed as a day at the beach. On other days, I struggled as if in the throes of childbirth. Time after time, when a creative thought randomly popped into my head, I'd rush to the PC before it hid itself in a deep dark crevice of my brain, never to be heard from again. Without fail, one of life's little everyday mishaps would stop me in mid-thought. Creativity would fly out the window, and once again the outside world and Murphy's Law conspired to turn me into a raving lunatic. Even on the good days, I battled self-doubt while my pessimistic nature cast a shadow over each successive word, sentence and paragraph. One thing was for certain; writing this book was no longer an absurd idea. Like that helpless child in <u>The Exorcist</u>, I had been possessed by a demon. Since I am a Baptist, and Baptists tend to be standoffish about such rituals, it was entirely out of the question to ask my preacher to perform an exorcism. I had gotten myself into this mess, and it was entirely up to me to cast out the demon.

"Who will read this?" A doubting voice kept repeating in my brain like a broken 45 r.p.m. record. Finally, the cloud lifted somewhat when I decided that I would definitely read such a book if one were in existence. Then, it occurred to me that there are thousands of other adult, female tennis junkies and possibly some men out there who might also see a bit of themselves in my gibberish.

It's high time that somebody, and it might as well be a nobody, writes a book about the not-so-ordinary souls who play tennis for recreation, socialization, consolation and de-calorization.

As you will soon discover, the book is written with a distinctive accent because I am, in the words of the late, great, Southern humorist, Lewis Grizzard, "American by birth and a Southerner by the grace of God." Amen. This is also written by the fourth and final daughter of a hero and his mate who are distinguished members of the "Greatest Generation." That makes me a bona-fide, card-carrying member of the aging but infallible "Baby Boom" generation. It is written with the well-merited wisdom that maintaining relationships, nurturing children, confronting failures, struggling to come to grips with loose skin, bifocals, varicose veins, cellulite, and the creaky joints of growing older are a few of the things that we must laugh about to keep from crying. If all that is not enough to get you on Prozac, then the stock market, oil prices, terrorism, snipers, and the real possibility that Social Security will be bust when we retire, should guarantee a lifetime prescription for it. You might have already figured this out, but to get through this life without mind-altering drugs, you have to be slightly crazy or you would go completely insane.

To my surprise, when the final word was on paper, it had become a table set with life lessons, self-discovery, and Southern humor, while tennis served only as the centerpiece. The stories purvey my personal journey from a barefoot tomboy to a bewildered young wife and mother to a middle-aged woman who discovers that her "thing" in life is the game of tennis. Ultimately, I realized that my haphazard journey is not unlike that of hundreds of other women I have been privileged to meet along the way. A select few of these women evolved into an eclectic group of confidantes, affectionately known as the "Volley Girls" or V.G.s. The passage begins many cans of balls ago on a makeshift baseball diamond in my aunt's front yard and ends in 2002 with the V.G. s' pilgrimage to the U.S. Open in the "Big Apple."

The bottom line is that this book was written for me by me. But, it could have also been written about you or by you, "tennis enthusiast or not." If not another soul on Earth ever opens its cover, that will be just fine by me. I will place it on a shelf and one day tell my great-grandchildren that I once wrote a book that chronicles my life and how tennis was woven into the fabric of who I am. Since Elvis is dead (although I still hold a fading hope that he's not) and I don't feel so spiffy myself, the certainty of it is not too terribly far down the road. I'll be silver haired, with shoe-leather skin and shriveled like a prune from curing on green courts under the Mississippi sun. (If not for the infamous humidity that goes together like peas and cornbread with the heat of the South, my skin would have scaled off like a reptile's thirty years earlier.) In all probability, I will tell my tale from the confines of a shiny, stainless-steel wheelchair after having total knee and hip replacement surgery. Years of joint abuse (the bony kind), arthritis, and inadequate warm-ups will have finally shut me down.

My young descendents will look at me in wide-eyed amazement and giggle, "Great Kay-Kay, (that's what they are going to call me) we didn't know grannies could play tennis."

"Sure, grannies play tennis. And, you know something else. If you don't watch out, they will beat you every time!"

Apologies are in order because, regretfully, I'm no Hemingway, Grisham, or Faulkner. At least, I saw it through, defeated the demons and wrote my one book. Before you start criticizing this compilation of words, I want to ask you something. Have you written yours? If you haven't, you had better get started A.S.A.P. because it dang sure ain't as effortless as Danielle Steele makes it look.

Love Doesn't Mean a Thing...

Reading this maiden chapter definitely will not improve your backhand or forehand, but it should give you a better understanding of the game of tennis and how it has become so popular. Before beginning work on this book, I had never really thought much about the history of the game that has become such a driving force in my life. I hadn't a clue how it originated, who invented it, or of what might have compelled the inventor to wake up one day and convince another person to swat a little, fuzzy ball back and forth over a net with him. In fact, nobody really knows the origins of the game, or for that matter, the country from which the game actually came. It is highly probable that the game of tennis was conceived out of a need to escape from the real world or as the by-product of a domestic misinterpretation (two of the very same reasons that I took up the game).

To my way of thinking, and if you are reading this book, you might agree that tennis is the greatest sport known to man or womankind. Tennis is not biased and does not discriminate against anyone. Period. It doesn't matter one speck how young or old you are. You can play tennis as long as you've still got that burning desire within yourself to not give up but to keep pounding that little yellow ball. It doesn't matter if you are big and brawny or tiny and frail, there will always be a worthy opponent on the other side of the net.

I've seen with my own two failing eyes, gigantic men, cocky with youth and powerful serves, brought to humility by perky senior citizens three times their age. I've witnessed first-hand two grandmothers "hang tough" in a third set tie-breaker and emerge victorious when threatened by two clueless college freshmen with thighs and buns of steel. In the game of tennis, experience, anticipation and simply knowing where to be on the court often have a way of prevailing over youth and determination. On the other hand, I've seen plucky ten year old boys give their teaching pros a run for their money during an hour-long practice session.

What other sport could possibly be so perfectly fair and non-partisan that even seventy-year-olds can compete with opponents the same age as their grandchildren? In what other sport do you find a playing field so level that even if you never picked up a racquet until the age of forty and had never dreamed that you could do anything more physical than take out the garbage, you can still get into the game? Tennis is not only a sport where the mind and reflexes are sharpened and the body is sometimes pushed to its outer limits, but it is also a social activity where lifetime friends are made. On top of that, it's more fun than skinny dippin'.

Although most of the time tennis is good, clean fun among friends who share a passion for the game, it can also be intense, "winner-take-all" competition between teams who aren't particularly fond of each other. Playing for fun, exercise, and amicable competition is what league tennis is supposed to be about, but there's nothing quite as gratifying as a nasty grudge match between archrivals.

Tennis is the most extreme, physically demanding, gut wrenching and unprejudiced sport on this planet, but it is not totally flawless. This is a hard confession to make, but there are a couple of things wrong with the game of tennis. Although it is entirely too late in the ballgame to go back and make reparations, the first mistake that the inventor of tennis made was to implement the use of a net. The game could have been so uncomplicated, and so many more of us could be a level or two above where we are now if it weren't for having to propel the ball over that ever-present obstacle we call the "net."

The second mistake was that tennis courts are just a few centimeters too short and narrow. Discard the net and add just a few inches on the sides and a couple at the baseline and the sport of tennis would be as easy as falling off a log. Certainly, if you play tennis, you have noticed that, when you hit the ball long or wide, the majority of the time it is out by just an inch or two. An enhancement of the court dimensions would certainly improve most of our games but would have some repercussions and far reaching consequences. This would mean that all the courts in the world would have to be completely overhauled and expanded. The cost of such a monumental change would be enormous, thus prohibitive for most facilities. Since the International Tennis Federation would never even consider such a radical change, it's best that the tennis hierarchy leave everything about the sport of tennis the same as its been for the past one hundred years. We hackers will just have to learn to keep the ball within the precious little space that we have been given and to be grateful that tennis courts are as large as they are and that nets are only thirty-six inches high in the middle.

Tennis is one of the most popular games in the world. Millions of people in every civilized country in the modern world play tennis. Besides being one of the most popular games, it is surprisingly one of the most ancient. Some sports historians have traced the origin of tennis back to the 5th century B.C. when a Persian civilization played the game of "tchigan." Historians also tell us that ancient Egyptians played a game resembling tennis in a town named Tinnis. Then the Greeks got into the act and said, "No, no," we started the game. Some tennis devotees don't think the history of our game goes back that far, as there has never been any illustration or mention of the game during Greek and Roman times.

This is strictly speculation on my part and not for one moment intended to be sacrilegious; but since the game was apparently around at that time, it is remotely possible that some of our favorite Biblical characters might have enjoyed a match or two in its primitive form. If they did indeed participate in tennis, this means one of two things: God either ordained the game for all mankind to enjoy, or he allowed its creation as a temptation to be reckoned with. If God did indeed ordain the game, it's wonderful to imagine that there will be luxuriant, grass tennis courts sprinkled all over Heaven where we chosen ones get to play tennis forever and ever against angels who always let us win. If He didn't—well, you know what that means. In Hell, there will be flaming, smoking, brimstone tennis courts where the unrepentant sinners are forced to play the Devil (he's the best that's ever been) for all eternity without a single sip of water passing through their parched lips. The term "wicked" serve, backhand, forehand, etc., will literally take on a whole new meaning.

Most historians trace the origins of tennis back to the 1100's or 1200's in France. Just to put the antiquity of the game in perspective, let's look at a few of the events that were taking place about the same time. Technologically, the English longbow, the wheelbarrow, and spectacles had just been invented, and the spinning wheel was in common use. Genghis Khan and the Mongol horsemen conquered the empire of the China tartars and advanced westward through Muslim Asia as far as the Caucasus, thus creating the nucleus of an empire that would become, under his grandson, Kublai Kahn, larger than any the world has seen. About that same time in history, Marco Polo wrote of people in China using paper money and block printing and of seeing coal burned for the first time. Tennis was around when the Magna Carta was written and the Crusades (all seven of them) were going on. I would enlighten you as to what the Magna Carta and the Crusades were all about, but, unfortunately, I was absent from social studies that week with a case of influenza.

It is not clear if the game was played with or without a net in the 5th century B.C., but for at least nine hundred years now, players have been swatting some type of ball back and forth over a net. At first they did it with the palm of their hands (jeu de paume), later with wooden paddles (after the nobles decided their hands were too delicate to abuse in such a manner), then wooden racquets, progressed to metal racquets and ultimately to the high-tech racquets we are so fortunate to have in the 21st Century.

The game became so popular in the dominant nations in Europe that, in the fourteenth century after Louis X caught pneumonia during a match and died shortly thereafter, England banned the game altogether. It is rumored that if you beat Henry VIII in tennis, you stood a good chance of being beheaded. Nevertheless, "tenez" (meaning "to play" in French) fever continued to rise. In the sixteenth century, Paris was home to more than one thousand tennis courts, both indoor and outdoor. Finally, it was banned again in the sixteenth century because citizens were so addicted they ignored job and family in order to play and bet enormous amounts of money on the game (the ignoring of job and family sounds all too familiar). It was later re-introduced by the wealthy as royal tennis in the eighteenth century.

Tennis anyone? It was not until the late nineteenth century that the game, in a somewhat different form, began to take on popularity in Britain with the advent of lawn tennis. Major Walter Clopton Wingfield, in search of a more vigorous game than croquet for the leisure classes, devised an activity that was a hybrid of badminton and court tennis (which had existed for centuries). He called it "Sphairistike," Greek for ball games. What a lovely, all-purpose word "Sphairistike" is!! It's so naughty sounding and fun to say that I am going to incorporate it into my vocabulary and use it instead of profanity the next time I slam an easy overhead floater into the bottom of the net.

In 1873, he introduced the modern game and in 1874, he patented tennis equipment and rules for playing the game on grass courts. Wingfield's rules called for the game to be played on a court the shape of an hourglass (imagine what a nightmare that would be). People soon realized that they didn't need the Major's kits. Wingfield let his patent run out in 1877; and in that year the All England Club, the current home of Wimbledon, held a tournament using the newly designed rectangular court and a scoring system more in line with what we use today.

One source says that tennis was introduced to the United States in 1874 by Mary Outerbridge. She was largely responsible for establishing the first court in the United States. This court was on the lawn of the Staten Island Cricket and Baseball Club. There is some doubt as to who actually pioneered the sport in America, but other sources say that Dr. James Dwight of Boston is known as the father of American Lawn Tennis. The very first original club was established in New Orleans in 1881. Tennis caught on quickly and tournaments were held around the country. The game quickly progressed into the fast-moving game of skill that it is today.

Since World War II, tennis has generally become more unrestricted than it once was. In Australia, by the 1930's, tennis had become the nation's most popular recreational sport and Australia went on to dominate tennis like no nation ever has, or most likely ever will. Following the 1950's and 1960's, the heyday of Australian mastery over the rest of the world ended, and in 1968, major tournaments that had once been open only to amateurs, (beginning with Wimbledon) welcomed those players who had turned professional. This ushered in the Open Era. This event had been anticipated since the early sixties, and the end of what has been dubbed "shamateurism" further fueled the tennis boom which had already begun by the 1960's.

There have also been immense (and welcome) changes in the quality and type of equipment and clothing worn to play the sport. While I am sure there is not much that can be written in our history about men's tennis fashions, there is a great deal to be said about women's tennis clothing. Men wore your basic woolen trousers or knickers with leggings, long sleeve shirts, ties, jackets, vests, and even hats. Women wore the same clothes as they would wear to high tea or an afternoon soiree. High-necked dresses, corsets, and, of course, all those petticoats, must have made it almost impossible to move gracefully. I wonder what prevented them from having a heat stroke. Perhaps the ladies considered tennis more of a fashion show than a sporting event and didn't exert themselves too vigorously. The shoes were flat and made of brown or black leather.

Finally, practicality ruled and the big hats were replaced by boaters. Thank goodness, the ladies were finally free to shed most of their petticoats and the new shoes had rubber soles with white canvas uppers. The men took off their jackets and rolled up their sleeves. White flannel trousers, white shirts, white sweaters, and even white shoes made the players look very dashing and athletic.

In 1877, (only twelve years after the end of the Civil War) Lottie Dod won Wimbledon in a short skirt. This was not so scandalous as she was only fifteen years old at the time. But the lady who changed women's tennis fashions forever was French superstar Suzanne Lenglen. She had extraordinary style and flair both on and off the court. Her outfits, comprised of one-piece dresses, minus corsets and petticoats, shocked the conservative tennis world but created great spectator interest. She gave women's tennis the boost it needed after the first Great War. By the time she finished playing in 1926, sailor suits, culottes, and even Bermuda-type shorts had become acceptable. Another player, American, "Gorgeous" Gussie Moran made headlines with her hemlines, and more importantly, her lacy underpants. When you consider the attire that players such as Kournikova and the Williams sisters wear, it is safe to say that "we've come a long way, baby" in what is considered acceptable women's tennis apparel. Men's fashions did not change much, and even when shorts became acceptable, many players still chose to wear long pants. Maybe they had knobby knees.

During the past few decades, players have gradually replaced wooden and metal racquets with racquets made of graphite and other compounds to enhance play. After 1984, when John McEnroe and Pat Cash wielded wooden racquets in the semifinals of the U.S. Open, wooden racquets quickly became an anachronism, to the lament of some purists.

Love doesn't mean a thing in the game of tennis.

When you are first learning the game and trying to keep score, you wonder how on earth they came up with the scoring system that is in place today. One, two, three, four sounds much easier, but it is very mundane. The French are never mundane, so we are stuck with 15, 30, 40 and deuce. How the scoring system evolved has never really been explained. It is thought that the term "love" probably comes from the French word l' oeuf, meaning "the egg" or "zero." Another theory about the scoring comes from France, where the most common silver piece was worth 60 sous, and each of its four parts was worth 15 sous. At this time of the game, tennis was played for stakes, so points were worth 15, 30, or 45 sous. But, after coin denominations were no longer significant, 45 was shortened to 40 because it was easier to say.

To standardize the rules of tennis pertaining to scoring, equipment, and court dimensions, the United States Lawn and Tennis Association was established in 1881. It is now called the Unites States Tennis Association. The USTA follows rules and regulations set forth by the International Tennis Federation.

The four grand slams, or big tournaments of the year are The United States Open, The French Open, The Australian Open and Wimbledon. They are all two-week-long tournaments played throughout the year. The United States Open is played during the first two weeks of September (see the last chapter in this book). The French Open is played the last week in May through the first week in June. The Australian open is usually played the last two weeks of January. Wimbledon is usually played during the last week of June through the first week of July.

Just a Little Trivia You Need to Know

*** In 1845, the rubber ball was first used to play tennis.

*** The net is 3 feet high at the center and 3 feet 6 inches at the net posts.

*** Tennis was first played in its current form in 1874.

*** The first lawn tennis club in the United States was formed in New Orleans in 1881.

*** Wimbledon Championships have been played at the All-England Club since 1877.

*** The Grand Slam of tennis means winning the championships of Australia, France, England, and the USA all in the same year.

Now that you've had a crash course on the history of tennis, let's go back in time a few years to rural, 1960's Mississippi, when life was uncomplicated and being a kid was the best time I ever had. To comprehend where this nonsense comes from, you need to know where the writer has been.

A Road Ran Through It...

On an early spring day a few months ago while visiting my parents, I took a sentimental journey across a forbidden road into my aunt's front yard. To my pleasure, the seasons had changed while I wasn't looking. The newness of the spring air and the familiar smell of freshly mowed grass caused a flood of memories to pour over me. Those memories were as warm as the April sun, and for a fleeting few minutes, I stood there, totally immersed in what was once a "field of dreams."

About the same time that the major leagues started their spring training ritual, we would begin ours. You see, my boy cousins and their friends played Little League baseball. Therefore, I became a baseball player too. Where I grew up, little girls weren't allowed to play organized baseball or encouraged to participate in any competitive sport outside of school-sponsored activities. The guys allowed me to become an integral part of their training program. I was bestowed the title of an honorary Little Leaguer, a utility "man," so to speak, or maybe even a guinea pig. Whatever I was really didn't matter to me at the time. It was competitive and tons more fun than cutting out paper dolls, having my hair rolled, or any of the other docile activities girls were expected to take pleasure in.

The first day out, all the boys were quite impressed that I didn't throw the ball daintily "like a girl" from behind my ear in a high arc. I threw it side-armed, snappy and confident, as they did. So, they took a secret vote and decided to let me be a rookie in the outfield, mainly because they were a "man" short. I finally got my big break and a chance to prove myself. There was no way I was going to let them down.

After school during the week and on Saturday mornings, we would converge on the only logical playing field that we had. We lived on hundreds of acres of land, but most of those acres were covered with trees. My Uncle Terry spent endless hours toiling in his yard, fussing over his beautiful carpet of St. Augustine grass. Every spring he knew that the yard would be transformed into a baseball diamond and that his manicured lawn would be completely bald in five places—home plate; first, second and third bases; and the pitcher's mound, which wasn't a mound at all. The elevation of the yard actually placed it lower than home plate. There was one more slight problem with our field. The road that stretched from Sandersville to Eucutta dissected the outfield, about ten feet behind second base. This meant that the outfield was on the north side of the road up a six-foot bank that lay at an angle of about 45 degrees.

Having a road run through our baseball field did present a few problems, but our love of the game helped us deal with them just fine. We could play ball anytime of the day, and knew when the road would be the busiest. With keen ears and careful orchestration, we executed every play. The pitcher would call for silence from the mound. Only after looking left and then right, pausing a second to listen for the slightest hum of a car engine, would the pitcher wind up and release the ball. If the batter struck the ball, the play was on, cars or no cars. Even if one happened to sneak up on us, we knew we had an approximate ten-second window of opportunity to complete the play free from the fear of being flattened in the middle of the road.

My house was caddy-cornered across the road from that of my cousins. I spent a considerable amount of time and energy trying to sneak across the road undetected by my mother, knowing full well that she would wear me out with a switch. From the day I was born, my mother had a fear of my crossing the road and getting run over. If she said it once, she said it a million times, "Don't cross the road; you know you'll get run over!!" As a result, over all the years since I left my mother's care, I have yet to cross a road without hearing those ten words of impending doom ringing in my subconscious mind. My aunt didn't worry that much about her sons as they spent half of their childhood years lolling about in the middle of the road, and she never seemed to lose any sleep over it. Although they spent many happy hours frolicking in the thoroughfare, the boys never crossed over to my side because nothing exciting ever happened there. Four girls dwelled in my house (five if you count my mother). The only activities they could partake of would involve nail polish, sponge rollers, Dippity-Do or Maybelline. Unlike them, all the forbidden fruits of my girlhood were across that dreaded road at their house.

They possessed a virtual sporting goods store—Louisville Slugger bats, Rawlings baseballs and Ted Williams gloves—just like the big leagues. All of it was at my disposal if I could just steal across that outlawed road to the promised land. Eventually, after my mother grew tired of hunting switches, which had become practically extinct around the yard, she learned to cope with it by busying herself in the back yard where she couldn't see us. "Out of sight, out of mind," the old saying goes. At times we could see her peeking around the corner of the house to verify that we were still safe, sound, and free of tire marks. After becoming a mother myself, I now understand why she was so concerned about us. She is a mother. It was and still is her sole purpose in life to worry. If you are out there and tired of worrying, just call my mother. She'll worry for you, and you won't have to pay her a thing.

On that imperfect field in that perfect time of our lives, we simply played the game of baseball. In the process we learned a whole lot about life. As much as children are capable, we tried not to cheat and strived to be good sportsmen. Name-calling was kept to a minimum, although it is nearly impossible when your teammate misses a well-thrown catch. Each complimented the athletic prowess of the other. We knew that we couldn't be the pitcher or the batter all the time and took turns at being the hero. Being hit in the gut with a ball hard enough to knock your breath out is tough. It's even tougher for a kid to "suck it up," not cry about it, and keep right on playing. We'd rather eat a cow patty than be called a "sissy" or a "titty baby."

It's true that my cousins dreamed of making it to the "big leagues" and becoming legendary like Mickey Mantle or Roger Maris. Ultimately, that didn't happen, but they did become Little League All-Stars, while I only played vicariously and cheered them on from the stands behind home plate. Being a little star is a hundred times better than never being a star at all.

I don't remember exactly what I dreamed of while standing across the road on that bank waiting for the next fly ball. Perhaps I just wanted to be a competitor and become a respectable member of the lesser, baseball-restricted sex. Every child needs to feel that he belongs and have the confidence that he can do at least one little thing well. No matter what that thing might be, whether it's being able to throw a curve ball or being chosen first in a game of "red rover," it will stick with the child into adulthood and positively or negatively impact his self esteem for the rest of his life.

Of course, I play tennis now. There is really no difference in playing baseball as a child and playing tennis as a grown woman. Both evoke the same competitive spirit, the adrenalin pumping anticipation of what might happen next, the hope that you can do your best and not falter or fail when the pressure is on. Sometimes, when I am serving for an important match, sweet memories of standing at home plate, hoping for the perfect pitch, embrace me. It is my chance to be a star for one moment in my life. No one else will ever remember if the serve was good or bad or who won the point or the match for that matter. In the big scheme of things, it will make no difference at all. The world will still keep turning, and mankind will not benefit from it one way or the other. It is such an insignificant thing when you consider that there is war, starvation, poverty, injustice and unspeakable pain going on outside of the fenced-in haven you've created for yourself on the tennis court. But, you know the old saying, "It is the little things in life that count the most."

That spring day while reminiscing in our abandoned "field of dreams," I was compelled to assume a batter's stance between two towering pine trees where home plate once lived. Amazingly, after thirty-five years, the grassy earth was still concave at that hallowed spot where we young dreamers celebrated a thousand home runs.

At that moment, I was ten years old and full of the excitement of childhood, not a bewildered forty-six year old member of the "sandwich" generation, wondering where the time had gone. I pictured the most perfect pitch that had ever been thrown, chest high and a hair on the outside. I swung blindly and crushed it with my imaginary bat. My heart leapt as I watched it sail up, up, and over the road into right field, completely beyond the reach of the also imaginary outfielder. "It's outta' here! A homer!!" There were no cars coming from either direction as I jogged from base to base, deliberately tagging each one with my right foot, until I triumphantly crossed home plate one last time.

That's enough of this nostalgic stuff for now. Let's move the hands of time forward about a quarter of a century.

Karen C. Rasberry

The Worm that Broke the Camel's Back

What exactly do women do to maintain their sanity if they don't play tennis? That is the question that often pops into my head when I'm basking in the afterglow of a three-setter battled out in the oppressive heat of a Mississippi August day. Nothing is quite so satisfying as that fuzzy, warm, speechless feeling you get after a hard fought match on a tennis court that's literally hot enough to fry an egg (and your brain). Even if that fuzzy, warm, speechless feeling is probably the result of a mild heat stroke and dehydration, there are few things that can even stay on the same court with a fine tennis match.

Looking back, it's hard to believe that I had a life before I started playing tennis. In hindsight, it really wasn't the life that I had dreamed about in high school. There was my "job" as a real estate broker, (which is really a chauffeur service for nosey, bored people pretending to be in the market for a house), the family farm (not magnificent thoroughbreds or longhorn cattle, but 48,000 stupid, stinking, clucking chickens) and of course, my sporadically adoring husband and our two perfectly awesome children. My days were a non-stop merry-go-round of car-pooling to school, soccer, little league baseball, ear infections, enough laundry to outfit a battalion, neck ringing (the chickens) and sleep deprivation. There was no time for me, and by golly, I wanted the merry-go-round to stop and let me off! I don't want to sound selfish, and please don't misinterpret what I'm trying to say. My precious children were (and still are) the light of my life. Except, there comes a time when a woman has to take control of her life and start doing something for herself. It doesn't matter what it is, just so it allows you to escape, regain your sanity and fortify your well being.

Believe it or not, there is life after giving birth. Granted, I am happiest when my children are safe and sound and under my roof, but children don't have to be on your hip and under your feet every living, breathing second of their lives. It has been over a decade since I traded a diaper bag for a tennis bag and discarded my dowdy denim jumpers for sassy tennis skirts. My only regret is that I didn't do it sooner. My children turned out perfectly fine and show no signs of serious, residual psychiatric problems.

My son is now twenty-six, married to the most beautiful girl in the world, and has followed in his father's footsteps to become a doctor of physical therapy. It doesn't matter that it took him six years and 50,000 smackeroos (no loans, no grants, no scholarship, no rebates or discounts—just straight out of Dad and Mom's pocket) to get his bachelor's degree. Yep, we paid sticker price for that sheepskin. "Boys will be boys," and it just takes them a little longer to get "focused." Thank God he got focused when he did, or I would have become a patient in the state "nervous hospital," suffering from a chronic case of shingles or on government assistance living in a second-hand single-wide trailer home, wearing holey, dollar store underwear and hanging them on a clothesline for all the world to see.

He is my man-child with a killer sense of humor and blue eyes to match, my friend and a fellow "Parrot Head." When he was a wee toddler, we taught him every word to every Jimmy Buffet song of that era. In hindsight, it was a huge parental mistake to sing "Margaritaville" to him as a lullaby. No small wonder it took him six years to finish college. He was under the assumption that college was about beaches, boats, bars, babes and being barely good enough to stay out of jail.

I look into those amazing blue eyes and see so much of myself that it scares the daylights out of me. After all, we grew up together. He is me, and I am him. Giving birth forced me to pose as an adult when other young women my age were still happy-go-lucky college students having the time of their lives. If I could go back and do it all over again, which I can't, I'm almost certain that I wouldn't trade becoming a mother at such a tender age for all the cotton in the Mississippi Delta. Please indulge me as this next sentence sounds like one of those sappy credit card commercials. If you are a mother, you will understand and forgive me. The precious, beautiful child that he was and the remarkable, fine-looking man that he has become brings me a sense of pride that can be summed up in only one word—PRICELESS.

After swearing that I would never go through the torment of pregnancy again, eight and one half years later, we brought home a baby girl. That thumb-sucking, blanket-toting, clingy baby girl is now seventeen and has blossomed into a fiercely independent, gorgeous young lady. Although, she has a deep-seeded fear of being dirty (psychiatrists call it automysophobia) which goes along with strenuous physical activity and would rather have her toenails pulled out by the roots than play tennis, she is quite well rounded. We all know that children hardly ever do what we expect or hope they might do. It has taken some time and much patience on my part to just let her be her own "march-to-the beat-of-a-different-drum-self." I am at peace with the fact that she wears pajama bottoms and flip-flops to school and that she only polishes one nail on each hand and foot (always blue). She has the reputation among her peers and teachers of being somewhat of a "free-spirited," Bohemian type child. The truth is that she was born 40 years too late or she would have been the perfect "flower child" minus the drugs and other seditious behavior of that generation. I would trade any athletic ability I possess just to claim the talent she has in one of her blue fingernails. She is everything that I am not—artistic, brilliant, amazingly creative and of precocious musical talent.

At times I have secretly wondered if the hospital sent the wrong baby home with us in 1985. First there were three months of unbearable nausea (if nausea were a color, it would be the same color green as lime Jello), six months of engorged, itchy breasts, and the third trimester with her precious little noggin compressing a nerve that ran down my leg, causing me to limp severely. Strangers pointed, stared and whispered out loud why any man would make that "poor cripple thing have a baby?"

She simply refused to come into the world, so my OB-GYN smoked her out by inducing labor. She's been mad about it ever since. Seventeen years later, she still won't do anything until she is good and ready to do it. After all my troubles and an

17

episiotomy the length of the Southern-Illinois railroad, what I got was a female version of her father. The only differences, other than their gender, are that he's not as talented, and she despises fishing. This just goes to show you that pregnancy is like a box of Cracker Jacks. There's always a surprise inside, but you never know what it's going to be until you get to the bottom of it.

It's only a matter of time until she spreads her wings and flies from my arms. When she soars away, there are three things that she will take with her: a blue guitar, her yellow, tattered baby blanket, and my heart.

My intense need to get out the house and away from the children for a couple of hours was one of the reasons that I started playing tennis. But, it was my darling husband—my mate for the past twenty-eight years—that placed the last straw on this old camel's back. God knows he is the most sincere, hard-working, dedicated man in this whole world, and I wouldn't trade him for anyone (maybe Mel Gibson, but he has way too many kids). He married me when I was just a child because, in his words, "I was scared someone else would marry you before I had the chance." Sweet, but hardly a reason to take a child bride. It all happened so fast that I really didn't know what had hit me. One minute I was a bubbly, carefree junior college cheerleader living off Daddy's money and the next I was married and supporting my husband while he finished his degree. Marriage...bam...baby...wham bam...a mortgage, chickens, another baby...bam, bam, bam. (To uphold my reputation, I want it made perfectly clear that Daddy wasn't toting a shotgun the day he walked me down the isle.)

In the short span of a couple of years, I had become a wife, mother, chief cook and bottle washer, and the wiper of floors, countertops, tears, noses, and butts. My life's work had essentially turned into that of a "wiper." I'd run into old classmates every now and then and they would inquire, "What are you up to these days?" For lack of something more thrilling to report, I'd chirp, "Oh, I wipe things that need wiping." When I was voted "Most Likely to Succeed" and "Best School Spirit" in high school, I had envisioned something much more glamorous and rewarding—perhaps the author of semi-great literature, but never in my dreams did I see myself as the "greatest wiper of all time."

The word "workaholic" is a bit clichéd' and overused these days, but I am inept to replace it with a better one. The love of my life worked like a plow mule during the week, but the weekends were his time to unwind. Every hardworking man deserves some R & R; and I really tried not to begrudge his passion for fishing. Being the loving help mate that I am, I packed his bag, fixed him bologna sandwiches and even helped him harvest repulsive catalpa worms from the trees in our backyard. Weekend after lonely weekend, with baby upon my hip and a nine-year-old begging me to play ball with him, we would adoringly wave bye-bye until he, the boat, and his rod and reels were out of sight.

One Friday afternoon I made up my mind that my husband would have to decide if it would be me and his children or a stinky, slimy mess of fish. Our son was still at school, and the baby was asleep in her crib. The wheels began to turn in my head. There was no way that I was going to spend another weekend raising his children without him.

In a desperate attempt to persuade him to stay home where he needed to be, I shed every last stitch of my clothes, struck the most seductive pose I could stomach and stood in the bedroom window—"nekkid as the day I was born."

Nekkid and naked have two very different meanings. One possible definition of naked is that you are alone and unclothed about to take a nice, relaxing bubble bath. In a different context, nekkid means that you are unclothed and up to no good. In other words, I didn't get naked because I felt as if I needed to take a bath.

For a fleeting second he looked at me with a glint of desire in his eyes. There was a moment of dead silence and a touch vacillation on his part. In my heart, I have to believe that he tried to stay. Then he did something that I will always remember and will never let him forget for as long as we both shall live. He pointed at his bucket of catalpa worms and yelled loud enough for me to hear him through the window, "If I don't go now, they'll die, and you know how much bluegills love these worms."

As I mentioned earlier, that was the straw, or more precisely, the worm that broke the camel's back. More than devastated, I fled from the window and locked myself in the bathroom, hoping that he would have a change of heart, break down the door, scoop me off the floor, fling me onto the bed and smother me with kisses. When that didn't happen, did I cry? Heck no!! But, I called him names that are still spiraling at warp speed through space and time. In fact, those names I called him were so vile, I'm sure the Martians have intercepted them by now and have decided to never invade this planet because, "those Earthlings with breasts are just too danged hostile."

Then I took a long, honest look in the full-length mirror. The reflection glaring back at me made me want to cry. No small wonder my husband chose fishing over me. Giving birth does strange, grotesque things to the female anatomy. I zagged where I once zigged and my belly pooched out farther than my derriere. My once shapely legs had atrophied into dimply white appendages, not unlike big globs of Snowdrift shortening that my momma used to make biscuits.

Reminiscent of Scarlett O'Hara or any other Steel Magnolia done wrong, I dropped to my knees beside the tub and vowed, "With God as my witness, I will never be lonely and dumpy again. And frankly my dear, I don't give a damn if you fish the oceans, rivers, lakes, creeks and mud holes until they are completely devoid of any sign of gilled life. I won't be waiting in the kitchen for your return with a frying pan at the ready; and you can bet your last catalpa worm that I won't be nekkid."

One of my best friends had just started playing tennis and had asked me earlier if I wanted to get into the game. Excuses didn't get in my way this time. I immediately dialed her up and asked if she wanted to play—that afternoon. With a babysitter on the way, I dug out my old aluminum, Spalding tennis racket, put on some shorts that were the closest thing to tennis apparel that I owned and kissed my squalling offspring goodbye. And, as you might guess, the rest is not history.

It is much more complicated than that. My first mistake was that I didn't jump feet first into the fire. My adventure into tennis was more akin to dipping my big toe into a tub of hot water to test the temperature. Tennis requires commitment, faithful practice sessions, and lessons every now and then. The first couple of years, our team showed up for matches lacking all of the above and was embarrassed over and over again. All that humiliation made me hate the game. Thus, I entered into a love-hate, on-again-off-again relationship with the game of tennis. My second mistake was that during the time I became disenchanted with Mr. Tennis, I entered into an intense, love-is-blind affair with Mr. Golf. Unbeknown to me, it was a love triangle that would have to end one way or the other. It was beyond my power to choose between the two. Fate and a series of unfortunate incidents ultimately made the decision for me.

Karen C. Rasberry

Torn Between Two Lovers...

At times my heart ached and craved the fast, furious thrills, and the deep, hard poundings I endured during my early fling with Mr. Tennis. On the other hand, my affair with Mr. Golf was slow, seductive, elusive, melancholy—the exact opposite of my estranged love—more reason to put the past behind me.

My good friend, whom I shall refer to as Mrs. J., (she is a G.G., golf girl, and an honorary V.G., volley girl) was in the exact predicament as I—married to a workaholic husband, two perfectly demanding children, a less than rewarding career. Menial chores and no pizzazz in life were making us both dull girls. It's a little blurry how it all came about, but if my memory serves me correctly, the plan was conceived over a bottle of wine and the deep resentment we felt toward our husbands for leaving us home alone for the weekend. We agreed that one day those precious babies of ours would leave the nest, and we would be left in an empty home with nothing to occupy our time—no hobbies, no more butts to wipe, and with husbands who had grown old before their time. If it hare-lipped the entire population of China, we were going to learn to play golf.

The very next day we went to K-Mart to purchase the "goods": a top-of-the-line set of Dunlop golf clubs ($129.95), genuine vinyl, Nancy Lopez golf shoes (on sale at two-for-one), a couple of sleeves of pink, Spalding golf balls, and of course, enough tees to build a small cabin.

I realize that there are many fine golfers out there and that I am unworthy of even cleaning their balls. But, for those who are unfamiliar with the game, let me explain in layman's terms how it works.

1. There are 18 holes to be played in a game of golf.
2. Each hole, according to its length and difficulty, gives you a limited number of shots, called "par," that you should be able to put the golf ball into the "cup" on the "green." All holes are either a 3, 4, or 5 "par" hole.
3. A total score of 72 is "par" for the course.
4. A player "tees" the ball up on the "tee box" and is allowed to "tee off" only one time on each hole except the first hole, where one redo, called a "mulligan" is permitted.
5. In the "fairways" a player is never allowed to "tee up" the ball.
6. A player must play the ball where it "lies." No exceptions, except when it is in the middle of a body of water. If the ball does land in the water, you must place another ball on dry land at the point nearest where your ball entered the water and then take a stroke penalty. (As this can seriously escalate your score, just stay away from water at all costs.)
7. One shot over "par" on a hole is called a "bogey."
8. One shot under "par" is called a "birdie."
9. Putting the ball in the "cup" in one shot is called "impossible," or a "hole-in-one."

Golf is a very genteel sport with numerous rules and etiquette issues to consider. These are the very basics and should suffice for the purposes of this story.

Within a few weeks, we were hooked—obsessed is a more accurate term. We purchased inspirational books, instructional videos, subscribed to magazines, bought all the stylish golf apparel and talked on the phone like eighth graders about our new found love. We aspired to play like Juli Inkster, but our skills were more on the level of Goofy in the Disney cartoons. Not to be discouraged, we played on with the determination of General Sherman on his march to the sea.

What causes a seemingly sane person to go off the deep end over a silly game had always been beyond my comprehension.

Apparently, it is truly a form of mental illness, because when it happened to me, I didn't realize that I was suffering from a sickness far greater than myself. At one point our husbands actually became deeply concerned about our well-being. We played in drizzling rain, wintry sleet, sweltering heat and even by the moonlight of lingering summer days. Day after day, we battled the elements and the course, which was always victorious, and "par" was as elusive as all those balls we had sent sailing into the hereafter.

We became known around the club as the "Nine Hole Wonders." At least three times a week around 12:30, after the O.F. (Old Farts) had teed off and moved out of the way, we would blow into the parking lot, jump out of our cars in sock feet, grab our golf shoes and clubs, unplug the E-Z Go, and send gravel flying as we tore out for the #1 tee box. We could play nine holes quicker than a cat can lick his behind and had time to spare before we had to pick the kids up at school at 2:45. All the "old farts" loved us because we were the new girls on the course, and we gave them something to talk about. Even though we weren't exactly centerfold material, they had been gawking at the same old G.Q. s (golf queens) for thirty years and were right pleased when some new flesh showed up. The G.Q. s were a formidable contingent of serious female golfers who didn't exactly welcome us with open arms as the O.F. s did. As far as they were concerned we had trespassed onto "their" golf course and had jeopardized their longstanding monopoly on the men's attention.

Every once in a while, when the sun, moon, and the stars were in perfect alignment, and the golf gods were smiling down, one of us would make the most amazing shot we had ever seen. We would look at each other, grinning with wide-eyed wonderment and exclaim, "How'd you do that?" But, for every one perfect shot, there were hundreds of perfectly awful ones. We "topped" it, "shanked" it, "dribbled," "worm-burned," "pushed," "pulled," "hooked," "sliced" and painfully dredged up divots the size of toupees. We grew weary of making a mockery of such a noble sport. If our scores and self-esteem were ever to improve, we had to devise a way to make the game easier. So, one day when only a few other souls were on the course, we decided to bend the rules just a wee bit until we could become more confident and adept at the game. What's the harm in that?

Rule #1: Mulligans on every hole. Yippee!!

Rule #2: Tee up the ball in the fairway if a half dozen mulligans didn't advance the ball more than 50 yards. Happy days!!

Rule #3: After finding a lost ball quietly nesting in the middle of a curled up moccasin, we completely vetoed the "lost ball rule." FORGET IT! Don't even look for a lost ball. It's simply not worth suffering a snakebite on top of a heart attack. Just place another ball in the fairway where you estimate that the prodigal ball made its exit, and continue without a stroke penalty. Why did God create snakes?

Rule #4: You may move the ball a club's length or two or three to obtain a better lie, unless you are on the green. Cheating on the green made us feel too guilty.

Rule #5: If the ball goes into the water, place another ball nearest the point of entry and continue without a penalty. Ponds are for fishing and have no place on a golf course.

Rule #6: You are allowed three tries with a sand wedge if your ball lands in a sand trap. If you are unsuccessful, pick up the ball and discreetly roll it onto the green. Add just one stroke to your score on that hole. (Because the trap will look like you've been doing archeological excavating, be sure to rake over the evidence.)

Rule #7: You may score no higher than an 8 on a hole. If you really had 15 strokes on the hole, put down 8 anyway. If you really did score an 8, make the notation "H.T.G." on the scorecard. This means "honest to God" and can be reduced to a 7 if your score were over 100.

After several rounds of playing by "our rules," we gradually weaned ourselves, and to our delight, "honest to God," began to par a hole every once in a blue moon. Actually, we went on and pared or birdied all 18 holes, but never on the same day or more than two or three in one round. Let it also be noted that I made a "hole in one" on #10, but at the time I was driving from the tee box on hole # 18. It was a uplifting feeling to know that it can actually be done, even if it was the wrong hole. That should count for something.

To the groundskeeper that I knocked senseless with a slice on hole #3, I am deeply sorry from the very bottom of my heart. You know that #3 is the longest and most difficult of all the holes, and

I was just trying to avoid the water and that huge pine tree. I didn't even see you until I raised my head during the shot, which is the reason I hit you in the first place. It is the one thing we just couldn't master, but never ever raise your head when striking a ball of any kind! Rumor has it that you developed a violent streak after that and were sentenced to ten years in Parchman Penitentiary for manslaughter. When you are paroled, it is my prayer that you will have been rehabilitated and possess a forgiving spirit and not attempt to track me down and bludgeon me to death with a Big Bertha.

That tragic incident kind of knocked the wind out of my sails. As B.B. King moaned, "the thrill was gone." From that terrible incident forward, I was fearful to hit the ball if there was anyone within 500 yards of me on the golf course, unless they were behind me, but that was no guarantee that they would be safe from my swing. The hard truth was that I didn't know where or upon whose head the ball would land next. I was a loose cannon, an accident waiting to happen, and a menace to my fellow golfers. It was painfully clear that it was time to hang up my battered clubs.

Another contributing factor was that, sadly, Mrs. J., my partner in crime, had developed health problems that playing golf exacerbated. The vertebral discs in her neck and back started blowing out one by one. Like a pack of firecrackers ignited at one end, a chain reaction had been set off in her spinal cord. If she didn't cease and desist playing golf, the doctor said eventually every disc in her back would blow. He stressed that the pain would be unbearable and that she, who stands 5'6", would be 4'11" by the time they all ruptured. What a bummer.

All good things must come to an end. Such is my love affair with Mr. Golf. Even though it was for my own good, it hasn't been easy letting go of my old lover. Occasionally, after watching golf on television or after sharing a few war stories with Mrs. J., I'll dream the sweetest dreams. In my dreams, we don't need mulligans, no balls fly toward the woods into the bellies of snakes, or dive into the drink, or ricochet off trees, garbage cans or unsuspecting skulls. Each of my drives are long and straight as an arrow on due course toward the hole. Every hole is either a par or a birdie. Triple bogies no longer exist. The O.F. s wave, whistle and gawk just as they always did. The groundskeepers fearlessly ride their mowers up and down the fairways, grooming to their heart's content. Best of all, we are real golfing queens in my dreams; and Mrs. J. is still strong of spine, fit and 5'6" tall.

They say that it is better to have loved and lost than to have never loved at all. Although I know that I would still be playing golf with fervor if things had not turned out the way they did, it is the game of tennis that is now my one true enduring love. We have had our peaks and valleys, highs and lows, but nothing else in this world makes me feel as loved, as needed and as special as tennis does. Golf will always occupy a special place in my heart and a tiny flame will always flutter and flicker whenever I drive by the old golf course where Mrs. J. and I left a part of our souls, along with a few divots they are still trying to repair.

The signature song by "Ole' Blue Eyes" himself says it best, "Regrets, I've had a few, but then again, too few to mention. I've loved, I've laughed, I've cried. I've had my fill; my share of losing. And may I say—not in a shy way, when it came to golf, we did it our way!!"

Who Are the Volley Girls?

It is rather ironic that my husband, the one who unconsciously forced me into a life of tennis, is the very one that somewhat fondly originated the term "volley girl." As it turns out, over the past few years, I have spent more time away from him playing tennis than he ever did fishing. The rudder on the boat has turned a full 360 degrees. Although he is still an avid fisherman, more salt than freshwater these days, we have managed to strike a very workable balance between work, family, and leisure. If he wants to fish, that's cool beans, as long as I don't have to go with him. Sitting quietly in a boat at the crack of dawn waiting for a fish to swim by and swallow the bait is Chinese water torture for me. It just doesn't make good sense. If you want some fish, drive to the seafood market and pick up a whole truckload of them.

My husband says that it is relaxing to be out on the water away from all the cares and woes of the world. The part about being on the water is glorious, but it's all that bait, tackle, and the patience required to fish that ruins it for me. My husband doesn't have a thimble full of patience when it comes to anything else, but put a rod in his hand and he becomes a modern day Job.

You may ask if I ever really gave fishing a chance. Absolutely. I'm the only woman I know who can back a boat and trailer into a launch without jackknifing the whole rig. From what I've seen, this skill is an invaluable commodity among husbands. A woman who can maneuver a boat and trailer is worth silver and gold to a man whose fishing partner had to stay home and mow the yard. I willingly went fishing with him time after time and learned more than a woman needs to know about the sport until he started using trickery on me. He'd swear that he just wanted to go run the boat motor for a few minutes, drown a few worms, and promise me with those deceptive cerulean eyes of his that we would be home in a couple of hours. The happy little couple would depart at dawn for a little cruise and not return until dusk after I was sufficiently dehydrated, starved, sunburned, wearing a shiny new fishhook in my thumb, in danger of developing encephalitis and not very happy at all. Fool me once. Fool me twice or even three times, but you can't fool me four times and get away with it.

Whatever the reasons, fishing is part of what he is and it keeps him halfway sane and sedate. If I spend the entire weekend playing in a tournament out of town, he doesn't normally complain, just as long as he doesn't have to come watch me play. As he always says, "I'd rather have food poisoning than watch you "volley girls" bat a little yellow ball around."

The first and last time he came to watch me play was about eight years ago at the state play-offs in Jackson. Although he attempted to be pleasant and appear totally caught up in the match, the look on his face told the real story. For two absolutely miserable hours, as he sat there crimson-faced in the sweltering heat; he was a dead ringer for a nauseated Charles Manson sitting in a hellish prison cell waiting for his next parole hearing.

There is one valuable lesson that he learned from his mistake all those years ago. If I take my clothes off in his presence, he pays particularly close attention these days. In fact, he won't even blink his baby blues. He's deathly afraid that if he ignores me again I might take up something really extreme like skydiving or race car driving, both of which would cost him some serious bucks and sleepless nights of worrying about my physical well-being.

So, who are the volley girls? For one thing, we definitely aren't girls anymore. Girlhood is just a fond and fading memory. Way down here in the South, a woman of any age can be referred to as a "girl." My mother graduated from high school in 1941 and still refers to her female classmates as "girls." One of her favorite pastimes is reading the daily obituaries to see if any of the "girls" from her high school days happened to have made the headlines.

The term is used lightheartedly and implies that, although we aren't Spring chickens, we've sill got what it takes to play the game. Motherhood, time, and gravity have not left us unscathed, but as a whole we are all holding up pretty well. Thank you very much. If some mad scientist took the best parts from each of us, including our tennis games, and used them to make one woman, he would have created a near perfect female specimen and one heck of a tennis player. In order to preserve anonymity, no specific names will be revealed.

For the duration of this effort, they will simply be referred to as a V.G. I can count them on two hands, give or take a couple of fingers. You might say that it is pretty pitiful to have played tennis with dozens, maybe hundreds of women and, when it is all said and done, emerge with only a handful of friends. There are other women in my life who just don't happen to play tennis (bless their hearts) that are my true, blue friends.

If you continue reading this book, you will see that women can be selfish, vengeful, whiny queens. The same goes for V.G.s. The big distinguishing factor is that they actually like **me** (and the feeling is mutual) despite my selfish, hateful, whiny ways. Let me pitch the biggest hissy fit you have ever seen on the tennis court, throw my racquet and act like John McEnroe, and one or all of them will be dialing me up wanting to know what in the hee-haw is wrong with me. They know when to keep their distance and precisely the right moment to confront my deplorable behavior.

V.G. s know me better than I know myself. V.G. s listen when no one else will. When I was absolutely convinced that I was dying from colon cancer and had only a few months to live, who came to the hospital to hold my hand and make sure I didn't say anything incriminating while under the effects of anesthesia? A V.G. did. V.G. s remember my birthday, come to the rescue when I'm drowning in self-pity, and make me laugh when crying would be much more fun. They let me know when my skirt is too short or when I have "radar" or when my roots need touching up. They know my phone numbers by heart and call them on a regular basis.

Like clockwork, on Monday and Thursday nights, the phone will ring. Since I am no Betty Crocker, they know if they call and I say that I have something in the oven that needs checking, that's code for "I'm doing my wifely duty right now so he won't be bent out of shape when I play in the tournament this weekend. I'll call back in thirteen minutes or less."

Any member of my family can glance at the caller I.D. and immediately announce, "It's a volley girl, get it Mom." V.G. s care about my children and try to keep up with their doings as much as possible. If one of us is going over a few bumps in the road with our spouse or children, there is always another one who can offer her wisdom on the subject because she has already walked down the same path in her life. We have our own little support group and, as far as I know, none of us have required therapy.

We are a curious lot with varied backgrounds and colorful personalities. As a whole we are a pretty special group. Individually, our demographics and vital statistics are much the same as the rest of the female population. Because the USTA requires birth dates on the team roster, our ages are public record. Our average age is 39.5 years. Whew!! Thirty-nine and holding. Unless we add a nineteen-year-old girl to our ranks, I'm afraid we will officially be "over the hill" by next season. This is just an educated guess, because a woman never really knows another woman's true weight unless she voluntarily gives out that information. On the average, we tip the scales at a remarkably trim 129 lbs, depending on the time of the month and how much we eat on any given day. Our average height of 5ft. 4 and ½ inches would have been greater if it had not been for me and my short self. Motherhood and tennis are the two main things that we have in common. On average, our households enjoy or did enjoy the pitter-patter of 4.2 feet and the totally wild chaos of 2.1 children.

We all suffer from mysterious, contagious, transient aches and pains. One week it's in the neck, the next thing you know it's migrated to the back, the next week it's moved on down to the knees through the feet and on to the next V.G. During warm-ups we sound like a bowl of Rice Krispies, with all that snap, crackling and popping that our old joints are doing in protest.

None of the V.G. s could pose for "Playboy" and wouldn't even if by some fluke the magazine sent us invitations and the promise of big bucks to appear in their "Real Women of Tennis" spread. We no longer walk around in the body of a college freshman, but our minds can still recall what it was like. We've "been there—done that" and it's very overrated. Wearing short skirts, Keddies and tennis shoes makes us feel young, spirited, and alive again. We may not be young and firm any more, and a couple of us are even grandmothers, but as the old saying goes, "It's mind over matter. If you don't mind, it don't matter." As with fine wine, aging definitely has its advantages, although we are hard pressed at times to pinpoint what they might be. We are in the process of compiling a list of the ten best things about getting older. So far, our list reads like this:

1. We'd rather be old than pregnant.
2. We don't have to shave our legs as often because nobody's looking at them anyway.
3. If we forget the score during a match, we can blame it on our failing memory.
4. If we make a bad call, we can blame it on our deteriorating eyesight.
5. We can use our advanced age as an excuse to not play singles.

As of this writing, we have been unable to come up with five more good things about getting older, but are diligently looking and hoping.

To give you an idea of how wonderfully diverse we are, here is a sketch of each V.G. in no particular order:

V.G. #1 ciphers numbers all day but can't divide a lunch ticket by two, a backboard, never shuts her mouth, even when she's playing a match, great naturally curly hair, she attracts men like bees to honey.

V.G. #2 works in the radio industry when they can keep her off the tennis court, has awesome angled volleys, never eats except when she's playing tennis, outspoken Italian, Catholic girl, considered becoming a nun until she met a man in uniform.

V.G. #3 is our Florence Nightingale, pulls magic shots out of her wazoo, giggles like a little girl, married a "coonie," thinks Fat Tuesday should be declared a national holiday.

V. G. #4 makes a killin' selling mobile homes, can take your head off at the net with her left-handed forehand, great skin, nice bod, runs down balls and drives her big red truck at the speed of light.

V.G. #5 works with abused children, her game is "steady as she goes," drives us to matches in her Astro Van, wears pajama bottoms to practice in the winter, our "mother hen."

V.G. #6 married a lawyer, so she works out every day, unbelievable "down the line" shots, prefers the finer things in life, loves country music and Ole Miss, a stereotypical Southern Belle with a just a hint of a wild side.

V.G. #7 deals in drugs, great volley, drinks a six-pack of Tab during each match, quiet and reserved until you give her an alcoholic beverage, only V.G. who plays competitive doubles with her husband, bless her heart.

V.G. #8 is a talented artist, her shots are all finesse and style, an all-American blonde, doesn't cuss, drink or talk trash about anybody, a lady in all respects. How she tolerates us, no one knows.

V.G. #9 wheels and deals in the used car business, never sold a car to anyone who didn't deserve it, great second serve, drinks a little beer before every match for "nerves," likes sex, busted the springs on two mattresses last year.

V.G. #10 is a starving writer and real estate broker, couldn't give a house to a homeless family, quick hands, slow mind, loves the net, a very sore loser, has been called "the rabbit" and "Tigger."

V.G. #11 labors in the legal profession, will lob you to 'til your tongue wags, can win a match without breaking a sweat, has an enviable, tiny body and a "bubble booty," loves to build houses she hates.

V.G. #12 works in the diesel trucking business, loves race cars and the men that drive them, swings hard just in case she hits the ball, half German, but loves Mexican food, has a thing for men with big quads.

V.G.#13 is a domestic engineer, actually likes her husband, squats and sticks her butt out as she simultaneously slams the ball down the middle for a winner, changes hair color a different shade of red weekly, could work at Hooters.

V.G.#14 works with teeth, has great ball placement, bird legs, nicknamed "Little," owns a billboard smile, a teetotaler, but has been known to dance for dollars after drinking iced tea.

V.G.#15 works for the "goverment," will return the best shot you've got or will bust a gut trying, epitomizes the term "team player," a Choctaw Indian, we treat her really nice because we don't ever want her to go on the "warpath."

My juvenile impressions of tennis and who plays the game have been scattered to the wind. Not all tennis players are wealthy. My middle class status is a prime example of the fact that you don't have to have a lot of dough to play the game. Not all tennis players drive Mercedes, own vacation homes and live in the lap of pampered luxury. Some are professionals with very demanding careers and a long string of credentials behind their names. Others work part-time at regular jobs or have already retired. Only one or two of us don't have to work (not me) and probably never will if they play their cards right. We love them anyway and give them advice about how to spend all that money.

Are the V.G. s affluent? A couple do fit the stereotype. Spoiled? Nope. Whiny? Hardly ever. Selfish? Only when we want something. Bitchy? When provoked. Vengeful? Only when it comes to tennis. Faithful friends? Until the bitter end.

For better or worse, for richer or poorer, all of the V.G. s are married or engaged and plan to stay that way. One of the V.G. s' theory on marriage is, and most all of us agree, "It's not perfect. The red-hot passion has sort of died down to dozing off to Fox News by lamplight. But, I'm too tired and too old to start over with training another husband. Tennis is more fun than red-hot sex anyway, and some of those anchormen are pretty darn sexy. Plus, you don't have to take your clothes off to play tennis."

If we all didn't love the game of tennis, would we still be friends? Yes, without a doubt! Tennis is just the whipped cream on top of our friendship cake.

Karen C. Rasberry

If Winning Isn't Everything, Then Why Do We Keep Score?

Over the years, I have played tennis with scores of different women and men. Twenty years ago in the rural South tennis players were a rare breed. As far as I knew, tennis was a sport played exclusively by the wealthy or upper class members of society. While growing up in the piney woods of Mississippi, the only tennis name I knew was Billie Jean King until Chris Evert, with her all-American good looks, came onto the scene. It was unimaginable that a middle-class, country girl who frolicked around barefoot all summer could become obsessed with the "exclusive" game of tennis. There were just a few courts in the nearest city, and I never even set foot on one until I was eighteen years old.

Thank goodness that it is never too late to take up the game, or at my age, I would already have been sentenced to life in outlet malls searching for polyester pants with elastic waists and floral house dresses or pathetically wasting my time in a smoky bingo parlor somewhere eagerly waiting to yell "BINGO!!"

Tennis is a timeless sport where age, sex, athletic ability and social class are all irrelevant. Tennis players come in all ages, shapes, sizes, colors, temperaments, and personalities. How we all mesh together to make a team is a constant source of amusement and never ceases to stretch the imagination and try the patience of team captains. Some personalities jive, others don't. It doesn't take long to figure out who is your true friend and only a little bit longer to determine who is a backstabber.

Women, myself included, can be vicious, vengeful, whiny, self-proclaimed queens who think the world revolves around them, and everyone else is just living in it. Throw nine or ten of us together on a tennis team, and you've got the makings of a regular soap opera or a hard court version of "Mutiny on the Bounty." This one doesn't want to play with that one because "she said that they said that she said I wouldn't move my feet." "That bitch tried to hit me right in the face with a volley. She didn't have to do that. After all, it is only practice. You just wait, the next time we play, I'm gonna knock her Bolle's and that ugly pink lipstick right off her face." Or, "My last serve at ad was good and she knows it. From now on, if her serve's not even close, it's O-U-T."

As a former beleaguered captain, I've heard it a thousand times, "Why do I have to play singles all the time? Why don't some of the others do it for a change? You better not sacrifice us at #1. We are tired of that crap. If you will remember, we played there last time.O.K., I'll do it, but don't blame me if we lose." Or if we are at district championships, the most pressing question is, "Are we here to win, or are we here to "have fun?" Winning is a heck of a lot more fun than losing, so why not sacrifice some lambs and go for the win? It's a hard decision for a captain to make since feelings will be bruised no matter what the decision, so why not roll the dice and gamble for the whole thing?

When winning is the only thing that matters, it's time to step back and re-evaluate the situation. Are you playing for the love of the game, or are you playing strictly for blood? One of the volley girls works with abused children and is the only women I know who plays purely for pleasure. She has seen more than her share of the heartbreaking side of life in her work with those children. She is one of the most sincere and grounded women I have had the pleasure to know and a fine tennis player to boot. Because she doesn't give a hoot about the latest tennis fashions, she'll show up for practice in her favorite Bermuda shorts and a comfy tie-dyed t-shirt. Her perspective on the whole tennis thing is this: "Nobody's paying me to come out here and do this. Why get bent out of shape over losing a match or all wound up over winning? It's only a game. Come to work with me one day, and I'll show you something to get upset about." Just last week she said she was thinking about buying a tennis skirt. We discouraged her from doing such a ridiculous thing. We are all afraid that if she starts wearing tennis skirts that she might develop an "attitude" and the same must-win mentality that plagues the rest of us on a regular basis.

When winning at all costs is all that matters, it's time to start separating the Volley Girls from rest of the selfish, bloodthirsty, whiny tennis divas. I love competition and winning as much as the next person, but the sport of tennis has taught me that you can't win all the time and even if you do, others will despise you for it.

When an activity that is supposed to be filled with laughter and camaraderie turns to tears and shattered friendships, it's really time to step back and seriously evaluate the situation. The only time I ever cried over losing a match was about eight years ago (the last time my husband came to spectate) in the district play-offs. Our team, the "Go Girls" (as in, you go girl!!) was 2-2, and our dreams of reaching the finals were riding on my partner and me. We had already played two matches that day in ninety plus temperatures. The score was 3-5, my service game. When my partner handed me the balls she said, "You can do it, girl. Hold here and we've got a chance." Salty tears of defeat were already flowing down my face. I was so dehydrated, that it's hard to believe there was enough fluid left in me to even make tears. "No, I can't do it, I'm fixing to die right here on this court." Obviously I didn't croak, but that match forced me to try to put the whole tennis thing into perspective. I kept telling myself over and over, "it's only a little thing." If it's only a little thing, why do I still remember that one match above all others, and why does losing it still sting so much after all this time?

The second and final time I cried over tennis was when I got left off a team by the very friend who got me hooked on it in the first place. I didn't shed just a few tears—it was a whole bathtub full—and they flowed for days. By the way I was carrying on, you would have thought that a dear friend had passed away. In essence, she had. A long-term friendship had been murdered in the name of tennis. She wasn't just a "chit-chat while standing in the grocery check-out line" sort of friend. She was a "double-dated in college, cheered together, tea girl in my wedding, saw Elvis together, know what you look like naked, deep-dark-secret-sharing" sort of friend. The bitter taste of betrayal stayed in my mouth for over a year and to this day still rises up in my throat.

The whole thing got so blown out of proportion that three-fourths of the tennis players in town got involved in the heat of battle. It was a battle of the betrayed and their sympathizers against the betrayers and their allies. We were cackling and clucking and feathers were flying as if a fox had just raided the hen house. The situation was ugly, ludicrous and uncomfortable to be in. Betrayal by a teammate who has been your soul mate for over a decade is a hard pill to swallow. Behind the tears, I swore that revenge would be mine and that "what goes around, comes around."

Eventually, revenge was mine when our rag-tag team played her "dream team" in a highly awaited showdown match. Expecting to see some hair pulling, name-calling or better yet, blood-letting, half of the club membership showed up and had a pre-game tailgating extravaganza before the match. We were the underdogs and ultimately did lose the match 1-2, but not before my partner (who had also gotten the boot) and I opened up a fifty-five gallon drum of "whoop ass" and poured it all over "Miss I Am Better Than You" and her partner.

Our celebration lasted late into the night and continued over the next several days. We even received bouquets of balloons and congratulatory cards from sympathizers who understood the enormity of such a win. The best gift of all was something I thought of all by myself. People still talk about it to this day. At the time, one of the V.G. s, who just loves to be in the middle of nonsense, was manager of a car dealership. I called her up and asked her if she had any drums in the shop that they weren't using. Sure, and she had paint and the manpower to get the job done. When my partner arrived home from work the next afternoon, sitting in her driveway was a pumpkin orange, fifty-five gallon drum with the words "WHOOP ASS" brazenly painted in bright blue lettering. We posed for pictures and generally had ourselves a joyous time with the victory drum. Over the next few weeks, until it finally disappeared, the "Whoop Ass" drum mysteriously turned up like a bad penny at a victor's house after a surprising win.

And, what do you know, when the celebrating finally died down, the sweet taste of revenge was not as delicious as I imagined it would be. Consequently, was I a better or worse person as a result? Both—I think. That little episode taught me to "never say never," and to keep the words "sorry" and "forgive" in my vocabulary. It also taught me not to simmer in the juice of revenge, or I just might drown in my own victory drum.

Karen C. Rasberry

It's Your Thing, Do What You Wanna Do...

What exactly do other women do for fun and exercise if they don't play tennis? You have already read about my aborted attempt at playing golf. For five whole years, golf was such an omnipresent force in my life that it is hard to talk about it without tearing up. Although time has helped heal some of the pain, I still bare deep scars from that failed love affair.

Gardening, flower and vegetable, is enormously popular here in the South and would be delightful if you happen to possess a green thumb. My thumb just so happens to be black like one that has suffered a severe case of frostbite. My beloved mother-in-law has a vegetable garden that I'm no longer allowed to set foot in when it's sowing time. In an effort to show her that I am not a worthless, tennis-playing, non-domesticated wife who is incapable of baking homemade biscuits and sends her son to work in shirts with stained armpits, I once helped my mother-in-law plant squash. What do you know—those seeds never even sprouted from the dark, rich earth in her backyard. That had never happened to her in sixty-five years of planting, so she naturally assumed that I was the culprit. Since it's apparently a sin to buy it at the grocery store, we sure did miss having fried squash that summer.

Marathon running would certainly keep you ridiculously fit and thin as a runway model, but twenty-six miles is such a terribly long distance to run. Heck, it makes my back stiff just to drive that far. A couple of years ago another V.G. and I got all fired up about participating in a 5K run that would provide toys for children at Christmas. In preparation, approximately two weeks before, we trained faithfully about four days out of both those weeks. It was apparent from the get-go that we were way out of our league. When they fired the starting gun, all the other runners took off in such a hurry that the air stream they created almost sucked our panties off. We hadn't even made it halfway through the course before we started meeting them heading back to the finish line. Once again, they sucked our panties back in the other direction where they belonged. That's when we realized that two weeks of training wouldn't quite cut the mustard when competing with hardened runners. While bent over with our hands on our knees fraught to catch our breath and hold down our breakfast, we began analyzing why in the devil would two forty-five year old mothers of grown children want to embarrass themselves in front of half the population in town. It was all a huge miscalculation. We were doing it for "fun" and for the little children who needed toys while the others were doing it to win. Plus, we never took into consideration that the course was hilly, much more that it appears from behind the steering wheel of a car, and that we had erroneously trained on level ground. Honestly, that last hill just before the finish line had to be every bit as steep as Mt. Everest. Quitters we aren't. We dragged across that finish line dead last at 36:23 and 37:01 respectively but still won 1st and 2nd place trophies in our age division. Although it took me a week to pick up my legs under their own power or to get up and down off the commode without assistance, I count that cheap trophy of a woman running against the wind as one of my cherished possessions.

Aerobic exercise classes have been quite the rage for twenty years now, but there's no thrill in it—no competition—no surprises—nothing at all to laugh or cry about. Just counting—1, 2,3,4,5,6,7,8, switch, 1,2,3,4,5,6,7,8, turn. To help ward off obesity, there are always the treadmill, stair steppers, and exercise bikes, but they are so artificial and unfulfilling—like going to the prom with your first cousin. Besides, it's depressingly unnatural and pathetic to exercise indoors where the climate is always a perfect 72 degrees. Fitness clubs ought to do away with air-conditioning and then see how many people tough it out and keep paying their dues.

I can't even begin to count how many hundreds of hours I've endured trapped inside a fitness center only to escape from the "cage" feeling like Squeaky the hamster who has just spent an hour scratching and clawing on her little exercise wheel, stopping every now and then to suck water from a plastic bottle. After 30 minutes on one of those torture traps, there is no winner or loser, just a little beep and flashing numbers that tell you exactly how many measly calories you just burned (not even enough to burn up one yellow M & M) or how many imaginary miles you suffered through. By gosh, when I'm done exercising and sweating like a racehorse, I want to have something to talk about afterwards and something to look forward to the next time. Not once in my life have I been dying to get onto a stair stepper or treadmill. I want to know if my performance was great or awful or if my serve was working, and most of all, I want to know the score!!

Snow skiing thrills the dickens out of thousands of enthusiasts, but it honestly scares me to death. Plus, there are at least two major obstacles for those of us who happen to live in Mississippi. 1. It snows about four times in a century. 2. The highest peak, if you can call it a peak, is Mt. Woodall at 806 feet above sea level. In the Rocky Mountains, you can easily fall for 806 feet and still be a mile high in the sky. That's the honest truth because I did it and lived to tell about it. These two facts make it impossible to snow ski in Mississippi, so we are forced to travel hundreds of miles in airplanes (which also leaves me white knuckled) and squander the kids' college tuition just to spend a week at an altitude and temperature where it is possible. It is a fact that it costs quite a good bit of money to go snow skiing because I've done it three miserable times. It would have been cheaper and easier to have had a hysterectomy. Plus, I could have had about the same amount of fun and the reward of never having P.M. S again. I didn't love it the first time, but I tried it two more times because I thought it would get easier and more comfortable. Wrong again. The hassle and the fear factor never eased for me.

First there were the ski boots. Ski boots are about as heavy and cumbersome as a '67 Volkswagen Beetle. (If jail inmates were forced to wear lock-on ski boots, the escape rate would be zero percent.) Then came the ski lift, which is where I consistently took my first fall. Naturally, the fall, which could take as long as a minute to climax, never happened when no one was looking. It always happened in front of an audience packed with perfect little snow bunnies and magazine quality men with peculiar, nasal accents (possibly suffering from a chronic sinus condition from constantly breathing in all that dry, frigid air).

On my third and final skiing expedition, things were going surprisingly well as I actually swooshed (at a turtle's pace) my way down a couple of slopes leaving Ss' behind me in the fresh powder instead of my usual Vs' from the tried and true "snow plow" technique.

My skills were improving quite rapidly when out of the wild blue, I took a dreadful, ugly fall about halfway down a "green" slope. Bundled up tots, not long out of the womb, sucking on pacifiers and dreadlocked teenagers on snowboards were swooshing by at lethal speeds within an inch of my skull. My life flashed before my eyes as I lay there waiting for a ski to impale my brain at any second. While wallowing around in the snow, all tangled up like a Slinky toy, but miraculously in one piece, a paralyzing fear took hold of me.

My husband was attending a seminar down below in one of the resort hotels. There was no identification on my person. If I die here from a fractured skull how would they ever connect me with him? Where would he go to claim my mangled remains? Could they fit me into a coffin with a ski lodged crossways in my cranium and get me back to Mississippi before I melted? In a panicked state, but not so much that I couldn't realize that I must find a way to get to the bottom without really killing or maiming myself, not to mention the others who came in my path, an angel appeared over my shoulder. It was the ski patrol.

"Ma'am, do you need some assistance?" I wanted to kiss him but just about snapped his beautiful Scandinavian head off instead, "Nooo! I just thought I'd stop here and rest. Lord yes, I need some assistance!! If you will get me off this giant snow cone, I'll give you everything I own or ever hope to own, and I promise you that you will never see my sea level, Mississippi feet on skis again!!"

After he uncoiled and hoisted me up, he positioned me behind him with my skis between his skis and my breasts pressed against his back and my arms in a death grip around his waist. Off we glided as one down the mountain in that strangely erotic

46

position. When we arrived at the bottom, he said several times, "Ma'am...oh, ma'am, you can turn me loose now." For a split second I considered going back up and falling again, but the fear of dying and all the inconvenience it would cause my family far outweighed my momentary infatuation with the golden haired rescuer.

Snow just ain't my style. Believe me, I have mulled this over considerably and have decided that people born and raised in the South aren't supposed to ski. God didn't intend for us to be cold and miserable or He would have delivered us in the state of Colorado or Utah or some frozen peak in the Alps.

When I was in one of my frequent "artsy-fartsy" phases, I bought a second-hand kiln with the dream of creating unique, one of a kind pottery that would surely be featured in <u>Southern Living</u>. After painstaking days of working with in the mud, it was a little disconcerting when, within a few minutes, it sounded like a small war had broken out in my garage. Evidently, my wedging and kneading skills were lacking a bit, which accounted for the pow-pa-pow-pop-pop-popping I heard as my first batch of "masterpieces" exploded into a gozillion pieces during the maiden firing. Too many air pockets in the clay is what the manual said. Although the kiln now sits cold in my garage, waiting for the creative inner me to be reborn, that just about wrapped up that little Bohemian dream.

Now, you can understand why I play tennis. I have failed miserably at every attempt to do the things that other women might consider enjoyable and fulfilling. If nothing else, I consider myself a halfway decent intermediate level tennis player. Everybody has got to be somewhere doing "something." My "thing" fortuitously turned out to be the game of tennis.

If you are reading this, you probably are a tennis player yourself and have pondered the same questions. You might not realize it, but there is some innate driving force, other than the aforementioned failure to accomplish other things, that compels us to play tennis as passionately as we do. Whatever that force is, it sets us apart from other women and makes us special. You have your reasons, or perhaps you just never thought about it, but my obsession with the game also has something to do with the fact that I was supposed to have been a boy.

After having three girls, my mother was practically guaranteed to deliver a bouncing baby boy. It didn't happen, just wasn't meant to be. My poor father would have no son to carry his name into the ages. For a father with no sons, he expressed no regrets and made the most of the hand he had been dealt. We became hunting and fishing buddies, faithfully attended football games to cheer on his friends' sons and watched my sisters play basketball on the hardwood of the old school gym. He didn't get a boy, but he succeeded beautifully in turning me into one of the biggest tomboys south of the Mason-Dixon line.

In elementary school, I never quite seemed to fit in. I wanted to spend recess competing with the boys, which prompted the girls to whisper behind my back. After a particularly bad day at being a girl, I got sent to the principal's office for spitting Coke on a girl because she called me a "hermophodite" (fighting words that meant I was a cross between a girl and boy). Her name was Dorinda and she had tormented me for the last time. A fat, freckled, knock-kneed girl, she always had boogers hanging out of her nose and she needed to be spat upon. After the principal administered three humiliating whacks to my behind with a ruler, I came home from school dejected and depressed. At the age of ten, my life was over.

Admittedly, I am still somewhat of a tomboy and would rather mow the yard than cook a meal. In my opinion, a man could do much worse than marrying a tomboy. She can do, or at least will attempt to do everything he can do except pee standing up and have babies too. Actually, a woman can pee standing up if she is so inclined, but it is best to attempt it outdoors. She better make sure that her stance is really spread eagle with the pelvis thrust forward and that all clothing below the waist is removed and put aside. On the other hand, having babies is something that a man can't even attempt. Even if men could have babies, they would do it only once because they couldn't stand the pain. If it were left up to men to have babies, the entire human race would become extinct after one generation.

Put Down Those Brownies and Get in the Game, Girl!!!

Do women who don't play tennis abide in homes that are free of "dust bunnies," cobwebs, mold, mildew, soap scum and toilet bowl ring? Are their cupboards always filled with the makings of scrumptious dinners? Do their children ever stand zombie-like at the refrigerator with the door open waiting for some food to magically appear? Do they ever run out of toilet paper and milk? Do all their socks always emerge from the dryer with mates? If they don't play tennis and their households are less than fairy tale, they should be terribly ashamed or have a very viable excuse.

Some might inquire where we V.G. s find the time to play tennis. My response to them is, let the spiders weave their webs, let the dust bunnies multiply, pour some disinfectant in that stinky old commode, and let the socks find their own mates. One hundred years from now when you are pushing up daisies, who will care or remember that your house smelled like a cattle barn and looked like it had been ransacked by a pack of Gypsies? There is no better time to play tennis than the present. You are not getting any younger or firmer sitting behind a desk staring at a computer screen or lying broadside like a beached whale on the couch watching some mindless reality show, throwing back chocolate brownies like popcorn, thinking you are counteracting them with diet soda.

Tennis is strenuous, demanding and downright backbreaking at times. Tennis isn't for the timid, the slothful or the weak. Only real women play tennis. It doesn't matter if you can't hit the

Superdome with a racquet and tennis ball or sprint more than twenty feet without suffering from chest pains and shortness of breath. Everybody's got to start somewhere, even if it is on the bottom rung of the tennis ladder.

Don't be concerned that you won't have anyone else with the same skills to play with or that you will be thrown onto the court with seasoned players. The United States Tennis Association has seventeen sections across the nation. They have also developed an ingenious program called the National Tennis Rating Program (NTRP) which allows players of all levels to compete with other players of the same level. The NTRP facilitates a level of competition for everyone—from 1.0 (don't know diddly) on up to 7.0 (Venus, Serena, Pete, Andre). Call the nearest tennis center and talk to the pro. Practically every small to mid-size town in America has a facility where you can get started. Don't be embarrassed to give it a try. Take a lesson or two and don't be mortified if you swing and miss or get your feet all tangled up like a 7th grader at a Valentine's dance. We've been playing for years and still manage to swing and miss from time to time.

If you are worried that you will be guilty of child neglect if you go out and chase a little yellow ball all over creation, not to worry. As you have already read, my children turned out just fine, as have the children of all the other V.G.s. If your husband isn't particularly thrilled with the idea of your bouncing around scantily clad in front of all those oversexed tennis boys, tell him to go fish. He'll get over it; or he'll join you.

If he also takes up the game, let him play until his arm falls off at the elbow, but **never, ever** allow your husband to be your partner or opponent on the tennis court. Don't be concerned with this mixed doubles quandary at this point. We will cover this subject in greater detail later on after you learn a few things about women's league tennis.

Go ahead, pick up the phone and call a friend who is also chompin' at the bits to get out of the house and into the game. Let's be perfectly honest for a few moments. You Junior League types can only do so much volunteer work. After a while it becomes so demanding and life-consuming that you may just as well get a paying job and donate the proceeds to charity. Volunteer work is a very honorable endeavor, and thank goodness someone is willing to reach out to the needy masses. Not wanting to appear cynical or indifferent to the needs of others, I must confess that I've done my fair share of community service in the past. Once it all becomes a superficial excuse to get away from the husband and children, it's time to let it ride.

For example, what would your husband rather hear you say: "Dumplin', I am going to the club to play doubles with the girls so I can work some of this cellulite off my thighs," or "God, I've got to meet that floozy Tippy at the high school so we can teach sexual abstinence to a bunch of sex-crazed high school juniors"? Wake up and smell the coffee! Five percent of those high school juniors already have babies and another ninety percent are practicing. That leaves a measly five percent that might pay attention if you can keep them awake. You can preach sexual abstinence until your tongue falls out, and it won't turn that testosterone into anything other than what it's always been—T-R-O-U-B-L-E with a capital "T." "Love can wait." What a crock of crab dip. Tippy didn't wait. Let's be honest for one second. Did you?

At the other end of the spectrum, if you have a career and children and are about to lose your sanity if you have to drag home from work, cook dinner, do the laundry, help with homework and pamper your husband all at the same time, then finally collapse into bed at 1:00 a.m. one more time, it's time to make a new plan, Stan. Hire somebody to do the housework and place the pizza delivery number in bold writing on a slip of paper under a magnet on the frig. Call the tennis pro to set up a lesson after work. After he's had his way with you, I guarantee you will come home in a much better mood. You will actually be happy to see your offspring and your spouse. Those little endorphins that your brain churns out when you are exercising and exhilarated will transform you into a new and improved woman. Plus, you will sleep like a baby and probably won't even be disturbed by your husband's snoring.

After a few weeks, if all goes according to plan, you'll be hooked. You'll be hitting forehands down the line and backhands cross-court. You will learn to love the "net" and probably despise overhead drills. When you are not on the court, you will be on the phone day and night chatting with your very own clique of tennis girls about your newfound passion. Remember, it's not really the tennis that you are addicted to, it's those sneaky little endorphins that your brain is producing that are making you crazy.

Once you are hooked on the game, the next logical step of your journey into the world of women's league tennis is the absolutely dreadful task of shopping for tennis clothes.

It's Not How You Play the Game that Counts...

I'm not foolish enough to try and take on the role of a tennis fashion consultant. Most women, if their mommas raised them right, know what to wear for any occasion that might arise. Every fashion-conscious woman knows not to wear white shoes after Labor Day; loud, Hawaiian print dresses to funerals; Fredrick's of Hollywood to Sunday morning services, or any clothing that reveals your cleavage to a job interview unless it's at a strip joint or to apply for a Washington internship.

Back in 1972, my high school Home Economics teacher taught us that ladies should practice modesty in all things and the "rule of stripes." For example, if your hips are wider than an ironing board or you have to sit sideways in a dining room chair or you could sail a barge with your trousers, horizontal stripes are definitely taboo. Solid dark colors, preferably black, or tiny vertical strips would be a more flattering choice. If you were lucky enough to have descended from a gene pool that blessed you with height, long, willowy limbs, and a rump the size of two peanuts, even purple and lime horizontal stripes are wonderful. She also taught us the "fingertip" rule. If the hem of your skirt or shorts falls above your fingertips when you are upright with your arms by your side, the garment is simply too short.

In her infinite wisdom, she also taught us not to wear "cookie cutters." "Cookie cutters" are slacks or jeans so tight and ill-fitting that they creep up into that part of the female anatomy known as the labia or the lips of the vagina (the cookie). It's disgusting and repulsive, if you've ever seen it, especially if worn by those who also shouldn't wear horizontal stripes. Wearing "cookie cutters" for any length of time can cause numbness and chafing to that very delicate area of the body and your panties might have to be surgically extracted with needle-nose pliers. Sister, if you are guilty of this mortal, fashion sin, you must repent immediately.

The things we learn in are youth tend to stick with us into adulthood. Mrs. "D," my beloved Home-Ec teacher, can rest assured that I still try my best to adhere to what she taught me—on and off the tennis court. It has become painfully apparent that many other women didn't have such a mentor as Mrs. "D," or their mothers didn't raise them right—one of the two.

Instead of attempting to advise you of what to wear on the tennis court, I feel it would be more prudent and helpful to advise you what NOT to wear to play tennis.

Lingerie. Some of the better-known tennis apparel makers have started designing tennis clothes that belong more in the bedroom than the locker room. Some ditsy young designer, recently fired from her job as a designer of gaudy underwear, who never hit a tennis ball or sweated a drop in her life, could be the culprit behind all of this. Or more likely, it's a man who habitually watches Bay Watch re-runs and suffers from "Pamela Anderson Syndrome."

If you just spent five grand for a new set of double D's, for your mama's sake, don't wear lingerie to play tennis. Case in point: Last summer at a mixed doubles tournament in a nearby city, a Pamela Anderson wanna' be showed up in a slinky little chemise that could have fit into a lipstick case. Half the men in the complex called a let and just stood agape like horny toads as she sashayed by each court. She appeared completely oblivious to the spectacle that she was creating, but you and I both know that her primary mission that day was not to play tennis. It was to show off her new toys. The referee gave a warning for play to resume immediately. It was too late. The men weren't fit to kill after that.

My bosoms ain't much to look at and have not caused a single man to call a let, but I still want to protect them by wearing a sports bra that will keep them all snug and secure. Sports bras are about as sexy as an old maid's drawers, and they smush your boobs flatter than a pancake, but its better than jiggling and flopping around, especially during that tender time of the month when those hormones are raging. If you don't support yourself, eventually gravity will take over and they will resemble a pink tube sock with a softball stuffed in the toe swinging from your breastbone.

There is another drawback to sports bras. They are almost impossible to remove once they are soaked with perspiration because most of them don't have any fasteners with which to free yourself. They can weigh close to five pounds when wet and often form a vacuum that is nearly impossible to break—kind of like a chastity belt for the boobs. Be aware, if you have just finished a tennis match in the middle of July and find yourself in the position to fool around a little, you can forget spontaneity. If the irresistible urge to participate in some post-match activities strikes, your partner will be completely worn out by the time he finally breaks the G-force on your wet sports bra. In the heat of the moment, one of the naturally voluptuous V.G. s once dislocated her shoulder and gave her husband a black eye when her grip slipped while hurrying to disengage from a sweaty sports bra.

Since we are on the subject of underwear, let's talk a little bit about Keddies. You can never own too many Keddies and should always keep a pair or two in your tennis bag on account of you just never know when you will need a fresh pair. They come in an endless array of cheerful, bright colors and patterns, and in graciously large sizes if you need them. V.G. s prefer the stretchy kind without a ball pocket. Ball pockets can add the elusion of a couple of extra centimeters to the hips, and that's something none of us V.G. s want or need. Keddies with ball pockets are actually a useless invention. We V.G. s just stuff the ball under the elastic at the hip area because it takes entirely too much valuable time and effort to deposit it into the pocket.

Keddies need to be snug but not so snug as to pinch or pull in the groin area. It's very distracting to be constantly worried with adjusting and pulling on the elastic while you are in the middle of a tiebreaker. I've also tried wearing those longer mid-thigh tights, but they inevitably end up becoming the dreaded "cookie cutters" and can also make that meaty part of your thigh kind of gather up around your knees. If you have ever paid attention to an elephant's knees, you'll understand what I'm talking about.

Wearing Keddies that are too large is worse than having them too tight. When the elastic blows out of the waist and legs, it's time to just burn them because they can no longer serve any useful purpose other than a dust rag. One of the V. Gs made the gravely embarrassing mistake of wearing a pair of "droopy drawers" to play a match in the Mayor's Open a couple of years ago.

This is her play-by-play description of what happened: "The match was scheduled for 8:00 a.m. that morning and I hadn't had time to do the laundry. All of my other Keddies were in the dirty clothes hamper, so I grabbed the only pair left in the drawer. Lord, they were huge, but I didn't have time to worry about it at the moment. I was in a panic to get to the court in ten minutes." She's a size four and those Keddies would have been a perfect fit for Shamu. Her next-door neighbor also plays tennis, but she wears a size twenty-two (maybe bigger but not smaller). She thinks her dog somehow drug those Keddies from next door and they wound up in her washing machine and then in her drawer.

"Right there in front of the mayor, God and everybody, I took off running like a banshee from the deuce side to the ad side to return a high top-spin lob. The ball took a funny bounce toward the fence. I jumped up to return it and those Keddies dropped down around my knees." What did she do? She nonchalantly slipped them off, deposited them in the garbage can and kept right on playing with nothing but a floral Victoria's Secret thong between her behind and the rest of the world. She went on to win the match like nothing ever happened. Never missed a beat. She's a true V.G. if I ever saw one. There's a good lesson to learn from this: YOU CAN NEVER OWN TOO MANY KEDDIES.

Keddies serve the very practical purpose of keeping all of your "stuff" covered and away from prying eyes. Keddies are meant to be glimpsed in brief, seductive flashes—as in when you are tucking a ball into them or prissily bending over to retrieve a ball. If your skirt is jacked up in the back so high as to constantly reveal your Keddies and that repulsive white crease just below your cheeks, it's time to invest in some larger skirts, or just go on back to the house, turn on the T.V. and eat some more brownies— whichever you prefer.

Just a few more helpful "no-no's" and we'll be done with this chapter. If you are going to play tennis you must at least look like a serious athlete who is capable of playing the game. Never show up in full body zebra, leopard, or reptile prints, although these are fine for Keddies. Don't get caught dead wearing any article of tennis apparel adorned with polka dots, stars, flags, slogans, the words love, tennis, game, set, match (unless it's made by Nike). Monogrammed club logos are acceptable, but a little snooty for my taste. I would also steer away from plaids, paisley, hound's-tooth, checkerboard and psychedelic fabrics. Unless you are six years old, for the love of Pete, don't wear anything fashioned from calico, kittens with their bodies' contorted so as to spell the word TENNIS, frogs saying "Rip it," puppies, dolphins, butterflies, or bumble bees.

It would be terribly unfair to talk about what not to wear on your body without mentioning the two most vital body parts that make playing sports much easier—your Tootsies. Wearing shoes that fit properly, absorb shock, support the arch, and leave a gracious plenty of room for the toes cannot be stressed enough. It's advisable to try on new tennis shoes at the end of the day or after a match when your feet are at their plumpest and most tired. If tennis shoes don't feel comfy when you try them on, you can attempt to break them in until the soles are as smooth as glass, and they will still feel like you are playing in those wooden shoes that the Dutch people hobble around in. It's surprising that the homicide rate in Holland isn't astronomical. If I had to wear those wooden shoes day in and day out, somebody would have to die.

For forty years I went about my business, never really giving much thought to my toenails except to trim them when they started turning under or snagging on the sheets and to polish them "precious pink" when I wore sandals. That was until the large one on one of the V.G.'s right foot came up missing. If such a malady could happen to her, then most assuredly it could happen to me. Later, she found the prodigal toenail in the lint trap of her clothes dryer. The disengagement of her toenail is still a mystery, but the podiatrist said it could have had something to do with playing twenty four sets of tennis in two days while wearing a size seven shoe on a size 7.5 foot.

If you play tennis consistently over any period of time, you will notice that unsightly foot calluses will begin to grow in the places that endure the most stress. Although these are very unattractive and can become coarse enough to strike a match on, take my hard-earned advice and just leave them alone. Consider them badges of honor that only athletes get to wear. Sure, you can smooth them down a tiny bit if they start ripping your pantyhose to shreds, but don't take some hedge clippers and start whacking away. Be forewarned, if you cut them off, they will blister up every time you play until they callus over again. Once again, there is a lesson to be learned from this: Never take your toenails for granted and always be particular about your feet.

Even if you are an embarrassment to the game of tennis, you can at least take to the courts looking as if you just won the silver platter at Wimbledon. If you don't commit any fashion atrocities along the way, you will quickly begin to earn the respect of your teammates and opponents. Remember, through the ages, tennis has been a game of class and style. In tennis as in life, "It's not how you play the game, it's how good you look that counts."

Remember What Your Momma Said...

If you play the game long enough, eventually you will find yourself in a situation that requires first aid, an improved sense of personal hygiene and blessed pain relief. After criss-crossing the state of Mississippi in the pursuit of tennis, I have been caught in several sticky situations for which I wasn't quite prepared. What follows is the first-hand account of the Grand Slam of them all.

Natchez is a beautiful, soulful city that clings precariously to the banks of the Mississippi River. It is steeped in antebellum history and the traditions of the Old South. That historic gem of a city (it's two years older than New Orleans) also offers some cuisine that will make you want "to slap yo mamma." Some of the V.G. s can testify that the city also has the distinction of being home to one of the most primitive tennis facilities in the modern world.

The state mixed doubles championship is held there each September, and we are always quite enthralled with the idea of going. Two years ago, our team got into free-for-all fistfight with another team who attempted to disqualify us on the grounds that one of our male players (my partner and quite the young stud) was playing at a level beneath his abilities. We can play tennis and fist fight with the best of them, so it was our team that represented the Pine Belt in Natchez as the unofficial boxing and certified tennis champs of the entire district.

How we do love a road trip, being out of touch with the real world, fiddle-fartin' around in a strange town, and getting a brand new t-shirt that advertises to the whole world that we are tennis champions. Fiddle-fartin' around doesn't sound like a very sophisticated activity, but there is an art to doing it correctly. The V.G. s have the art of fiddle-fartin' around as finely tuned as a baby grand piano in Carnegie Hall. This art form includes but is not limited to, lounging about in our drawers in the comfort of our rooms after a match while fussily planning where we'll have our next meal, keeping an eye on the Weather Channel while strategizing for the next match, talking trash only about those who deserve it, obnoxiously reading aloud every funny greeting card in an exclusive gift emporium, smelling candles or testing perfume, trying on forty-six different tennis outfits, and so forth and so on. Having money to fiddle-fart away while fiddle-fartin' around is always preferred, but by no means, mandatory. If we do have immediate expendable income, we spread it around like a politician running for office. If we don't, and the numbers were worn off our credit cards the previous month, we declare we absolutely couldn't find a thing worth a fiddle-fart to buy. Have mercy! The food, the camaraderie and the whole tennis tournament atmosphere is more fun than a free trip to Disney World!

Never!! Do you hear me? Never, ever under any circumstances short of torture, tell your husband or significant other how much fun you expect to have. Always tell them that it is deadly serious tennis that offers the rare opportunity to play some of the best teams in the state, and that it will improve your game dramatically. Furthermore, tell them that you will be totally exhausted and in bed by ten and that you will be rooming with a nun who just joined the team. If he asks you what kind of clothes nuns wear to play tennis, tell him that Nike just came out with a new, "Nuns Can Just Do It Too" line of apparel. In reality, it's just a great big P-A-R-T-Y (spring break, pajama party, and tennis camp for grownups all rolled into one weekend) from the second the doors slam on your vehicle until you drag back into the house with that "I'm-just-worn-out-from-playing-all that-tennis" pitiful look on your face. If you ever take leave of your senses and admit to what really goes on at a tennis tournament, just remember, when your spouse makes you stay home and help him paint the house while everybody else is off having a large time, I told you so.

Back to the original subject. Actually, the main facility is quite nice and as a whole they put on a fabulous tournament, or we wouldn't practically kill ourselves trying to get there every year. It's just the satellite facilities that could use considerable improvement. Although we always hope for a cool snap that time of year, Natchez (or any other city in Mississippi) in September is naturally hotter than Satan's living room. Throw that in with the legendary humidity of the deep South, and you get a sticky, steamy brew that makes it nearly impossible to take a decent breath. "It's not the heat, it's the humidity"—no truer statement has ever been made. The air doesn't move in early September on the banks of the lower Mississippi. The humidity causes it to hover and suffocate every living thing that happens to venture outdoors. Even if a breeze did stir, it would be about the same temperature as an oven set for baking biscuits. One should be declared legally insane who would dare to even stick a toe outdoors away from air-conditioning, much less play tennis in such conditions. I'm not that smart, or I wouldn't subject myself to it; but I have deduced that I am in the good company of a disproportionate number of insane tennis players.

Here's the scenario and vital statistics of players: Saturday morning, 7:30 A.M., already the temperature is 98 degrees with 95% humidity, the majority of heads are heavy and splitting from the consumption of two gallons of frozen Margaritas the night before, some are "green about the gills" from hot tamales and that demon tequila, went to bed at 1:00 a.m., bolted from the bed at 6:15, no breakfast, black coffee atop raw, empty stomachs, couldn't locate tennis bag or water jug, grabbed racquet and flew out the door.

On the way to the courts, after my head had cleared a little bit, it dawned on me that my tennis racquet had been used as a mock guitar the night before (not by me) and that my bag was M.I.A. because it was left on top of someone's S.U.V. outside an eating and drinking establishment that shall remain nameless.

When several of the team members, upon the management's stern suggestion, failed to "hold it down," we were escorted to the parking lot by a security officer named "Buford." He didn't have a pistol but he sure did have a big stick dangling from his belt. An affable, good ole' boy, he said his momma named him after the late Buford J. Pusser, the infamous sheriff who gained notoriety and maintained order in similar seedy places along the Tennessee-Mississippi line by cracking skulls with a big stick. No doubt, one more "flim-flam blim-blam" out of us, and good ole' Buford would have lived up to his namesake. The last R-rated outburst of "Hotty Toddy" belted out by one of the tennis boys at the top of his lungs was when the manager finally lost his enthusiasm for the big tab we were racking up. By an establishment that generally encourages rowdy behavior, we were shown the door for showing allegiance to Ole Miss and for a little harmless table dancing by one of the V.G. s (a faithful Sunday school attendee) who never has and never will touch a drop of alcohol. Law-abiding, God-fearing people do crazy things in certain situations if the right ingredients are blended in. We refer to them as life's little "unforced errors." On extraordinary occasions, tennis players just start having so much fun they forget all about their raisin' and can no longer hear their mother's voice reminding them, "Don't forget how to act in public!! You better not go off and act like trailer trash. You know you weren't raised that way." I'm truly sorry, Momma.

Description of the facility: No water, no bathrooms, scorching sun, no bleachers, mosquitoes the size of hummingbirds, nets 40 inches high, six teams waiting to play on two courts, dandelions growing from cracks in the courts, large, angry fire ant beds against the fence and a squeegee that is engineered from a large, forked oak tree limb and coat hanger wire. The nearest bathroom is two blocks away in a service station where gang members wouldn't dare to relieve themselves.

As luck would have it, we learned that our opponents didn't even go to bed the night before. They came straight to the match (after a quick shower in their rooms) from the riverboat casino and had guzzled enough beer at the tournament party to float the very boat they had just disembarked. We limped victorious from the courts, but what a pitiable sight it was—sweating profusely, smelling like a locker room, our limbs ravaged by blood sucking mosquitoes, thirsty enough to spit cotton, noses fried from the sun, on the verge of dry heaving behind the Jeep, private parts swollen and itching madly after tucking a fire ant covered ball into Keddies, generalized malaise and severe aching from head to toe.

At that moment any one of the V.G. s would have given a hundred dollar bill for any one of these items: Ice water, a fresh pair of Keddies, some foo-foo spray, Advil, Pepto-Bismol, rubbing alcohol, insect repellant, sunscreen, Gatorade, Flex-All, Band-Aids, a chair, an umbrella, a place to pee, some wet wipes and an air-conditioned room. And, not one among us wished for a margarita. The consensus was that winning had made it all worthwhile. Afterwards, we made a Girl Scout promise to never, ever again be as imprudent as we had been the night before. As always, there is a valuable lesson to be learned in all of this: Be prepared. Adhere to what your momma used to say, and try not to let life's little unforced errors get the best of you.

Karen C. Rasberry

They Will Beat You Every Time...

So, you have now been playing the game a few months, been welcomed onto a couple of teams, you're taking a weekly lesson, winning a few matches and beginning to think in a queenly way, "Hey, I'm getting pretty good at this game, piece of cake. I may even get moved up to a higher level next year, or I'm getting so good, I'll just play up a level." WRONG, WRONG, DEAD WRONG!! I am here to tell you that you are not as good as you think and no matter how good you are, there is someone out there who is better than you.

In my warped way of thinking, what comes to mind here is the catchy little song from the '70's that was sung by Paul Simon, called Fifty Ways to Leave Your Lover. All the last words of the lyrics rhyme like this, "Step off the bus, Gus...make a new plan, Stan...don't need to be coy, Roy...just listen to me...there must be fifty ways to leave your lover...etc., etc." If there are fifty ways to lose your lover, then there are surely fifty ways to describe losing a tennis match.

Take it from someone who knows all too well: sooner than later you will lose, and that loss will be handed to you by the most unlikely of suspects. You will be completely unable to analyze how or why it happened. Don't blame it on your new racquet, the wind, the sun, the cramps, your aching feet, a high net, your partner, or cheating opponents, nor do you proclaim that you just weren't "on your game" that day, because it simply won't wash and nobody wants to hear your whining anyway. It will be so quick, painful, and humiliating that you will be at a loss for words or credible excuses, because sister, you just got: Licked, beat, creamed, smoked, pounded, touted, your lunch toted, your clock cleaned, annihilated, upped, romped, stomped, smashed, blown away, sent to the house, topped, outplayed, tore up, scalded, walloped, jacked-up, whooped, crushed, overwhelmed, overcome, overpowered, outlasted, messed up, reamed out, highballed, rolled over, torpedoed, sunk, skunked, nullified, blown off the court, burnt, ripped, twisted, plastered, eliminated, killed, skint', tamed, grilled, got it put on you, ate up, made a fool of, outclassed, wiped out, spanked, blistered; and to use the V.G. s' favorite term—you got a good old-fashioned, well-deserved attitude adjustment.

If you are at the top of your game, playing the best tennis of your life, be forewarned that the unlikely purveyor of your butt whoopin' is out there in the shadows. It will be akin to a hit and run car accident. You won't see it coming, and if you did, you would chuckle at the possibility of being blindsided by such a player. Although she won't remember your name or the score until the cards are flipped back to zero, you will never forget her name because it will strike fear and trembling in your heart for the rest of your tennis playing days.

Who are these women, you ask? Well, it just might be your "mother" because she will be old enough to be your mother. If you are getting on up in years as some of us V.G. s are, that means that she is as old as the Pyramids.

Your "mother" has already forgotten more about tennis than you will ever know. She was an advanced player with a wooden racquet when you were still wearing training pants and sucking your thumb. Although she might not be as strong and agile as she once was, the textbook strokes, the finesse, and the court "smarts" are still very much intact. Go ahead, smash the ball at her with every ounce of your being while yielding the latest state-of-the-art, graphite, long-bodied, turbo-charged racquet on the market. The ball will come back again and again and again until you are mentally and physically exhausted. She has the patience of Job and nowhere else to be at the moment and will hit the ball a thousand times to win one point. Her husband is there cheering her every move, while you probably left your husband and children at home with no supper, his lips pooched out and harboring a big case of the "reds." You will become a puppet on a string and she will be the puppet master. Change up your game if you can, or take the pace off in a desperate attempt to stay alive. It doesn't matter one bit to her—six of one, half dozen of the other. She will effortlessly return the ball with inhuman accuracy to any spot on your side of the court that she desires, give or take a couple of centimeters. Drop the ball short when she's at the baseline, then rush the net like a rat off a sinking ship. She will scamper like a bunny rabbit to return it in the form of a lob smack dab on the back of the back of the baseline. You'll curse under your breath in amazement, "How did that old heifer do that?"

After a while, the match will take on a surreal quality, as if it's not really happening—just a bad dream. Instead of being angry with yourself, you will actually begin laughing inwardly and then out loud, to keep from crying. When it's all over and you shake hands at the net, you will tell your "mother" that you enjoyed your spanking very much and will try to do better the next time—and you will have truly enjoyed it. Your "mother" has been the perfect lady on the court, exhibiting exemplary sportsmanship. She graciously complimented the two good shots that you managed to make and called more than a few lines in your favor, when Stevie Wonder could have seen that they were clearly out. You will have learned more from her in straight sets than you could learn from a tennis professional in ten years. After playing your "mother," you will leave the court a much better more humble player all the way around—guaranteed.

The "Go Girls" (all Go Girls aren't necessarily V.G. s) sweated, clawed, and gutted their way back to the state play-offs year after year, but always came home defeated and empty-handed. The state championship was as elusive as four aces in a row. Finally, in 1997 it all came together on a scorching, Sunday morning in May at Parham Bridges in Jackson. The gutsy 3.0 ladies team from Laurel prevailed over the professionally coached, omnipresent forces from Jackson and the Delta. They were finally headed to Chattanooga for the regional playoffs.

Sadly, I would not be making the trip with the girls. By some computer glitch, I got myself bumped up to 3.5 the year before and consequently suffered through the most miserable season of my life. Although I celebrated and wept tears of joy with them, it just wasn't the same. The fact that they had done it without me was what hurt the most. Secondly, my lifeline to the other V.G. s had been cut and I was technically no longer one of "them." They were the Mississippi women's 3.0 champions and I was nothing but a mediocre player on a struggling 3.5 team. Adrift at sea with no land or hope in sight, I prayed every night that the rest of the V.G. s would make a fine showing in Tennessee and join or relieve me of my misery the next season.

Although I wasn't there in Chattanooga to witness the mayhem and massacre that unfolded in the shadows of Lookout Mountain, this account of what happened is the gospel "cross-my-heart-and-hope-to-die" truth. It was told to me by the most articulate (motor-mouthed) V.G. of the whole bunch. Furthermore, a V.G. would never lie about such a serious matter.

With all their flags and banners a flyin' and white shoe polish splashed windows proclaiming "Chattanooga or Bust," "You Go Girl!!", and "Nationals, Here We Come!!", the "Go Girls" and their faithful entourage rolled into town. Their hopes and spirits were soaring as the first match with a Kentucky team neared. The "Go Girls" were higher than Lover's Leap atop beautiful Lookout Mountain, and in their minds, invincible. Nothing could stop them now. Little did they know, but they were about to stumble upon the beginning of the end.

For the life of me it's hard to believe that I really didn't witness the match because the picture of it is so indelibly imprinted into my brain that the smell of smoke actually burns my nostrils. What smoke? The cigarette smoke. The theme song for this match, the one that dances around in my head, is non other than Burn, Baby, Burn from the movie Saturday Night Fever. The two women playing at #2 doubles were tennis playing, racquet-toting infernos, looking for two kinds of butts to smoke.

The two unsuspecting V.G. s were very heartened when their opponents, each with an unlit cigarette dangling from the corner of her tar-stained lips, entered the gate. Being from the Hospitality State and all that, the two V.G. s felt that a few introductions, "where ya'll froms," and other niceties would be in order before the match began. Betty Lynn and Bobbie Sue felt otherwise. That's not their real names, but both had those double "Ellie Mae" type names so popular here in the South. Breathless and audibly wheezing from their short walk onto the courts, they plopped down on the bench, lit up their smokes and proceeded to take a break before the match began. Not knowing exactly how to handle the situation, the two V.G. s went onto the court to start warming up. After a few drags off the cigarettes, their opponents crushed them out on the court with the toe of their tennis shoes, picked them up and carefully placed them on a ball can lid for safekeeping. Instead of ABC (already been chewed gum) they enjoyed ABS (already been smoked) cigarettes.

The first words the women uttered were, "Let's git this show on the road. My ole man's waiting for me back at the motel. We'll serve first. You take the side facing the sun. If you cheat us, we'll follow you to the parking lot and cut your tires. You are gonna' wish you had never been born, ladies."

Not exactly regulation procedure for starting a regional match, but the two V.G. s were too shocked and intimidated to protest. The two lasses from Kentucky pulled their chemically damaged, conditioner starved hair back with a piece of pink braided yarn (the kind we wore in 1969 to make pigtails), turned their baseball caps around backwards, hacked a few times to clear their lungs and began serving the first game. They won that first game love, an ominous sign that despite their impaired bronchial tubes, it would be a dismal match for the girls from the Magnolia State. During each changeover they fiendishly lit up those same pre-smoked cigarettes, took two drags apiece, squashed them out and placed them back on the plastic lid, all in regulation time.

The score would have been 0-0, but ended up 0-1 because Betty Lynn had a coughing spell while she was serving for the match which caused her to double fault three times. Bobbie Sue then hit a home run over the fence into the official's tent, knocking over a bowl of fruit. The V.G. s felt dang lucky to get off the court with that one game and with their teeth and respiratory health intact. When it was all over, Betty Lynn and Bobbie Sue had a complete personality change. They acted as if the two V.G. s were long lost pals, even offering them a smoke and a beer, which was graciously declined. It turned out that Betty Lynn and Bobbie Sue had been all-stars on the Kentucky women's fast pitch softball team that won the national title in 1995. They had been sponsored by a large tobacco company that supplied them with all the cigarettes or snuff they could consume. They chose cigarettes because it's sorta' gross to get sugar when you've got a dip. Despite the warnings of the Surgeon General, smoking seemed to improve their performance on the softball field, so they just laid with them.

69

As they explained it, "Smoking kind of takes the edge off when it's a close game. It also keeps us from bashin' in the umpire's teeth when he makes a bad call."

They became infatuated with the game of tennis when they realized they could knock the fuzz off a tennis ball with a racquet if they swung with the same dynamics as a softball bat.

This is more of a warning than a lesson to be learned. If you run across the likes of Betty Lynn and Bobbie Sue, fake some kind of injury or gag yourself and throw up on the court. Then, pick up your pitiful pile of junk, and limp as fast as you can in the other direction back to Mississippi or wherever it is that you hang your racquet.

Now that we have gone over the fifty ways to describe being beaten by your "mother" and the consequences of believing that chain-smoking women cannot kick your butt, you need to be enlightened about one more annoying player who will also do irreparable damage to your self esteem as well as your fanny. This predator may be the hardest of all to deal with psychologically because she will not only whip your physically imperfect tail, but she will think she looks great and will keep you in a state of agitation the whole time she is doing it. Forget Paul Simon and John Travolta for now. Just close your eyes and hear Burt Parks croon his legendary version of There She Is, Miss America…imagine the runway, the crown, the tears, the Vaseline greased smiles, slow motion waving to the adoring subjects.

Every little girl at one time or another dreams of becoming Miss America. It is part of our culture. Little girls want to be Miss America and little boys want to marry her. If you deny that you ever dreamed of owning that crown and the adoration of a whole nation, you are lying like a rug and you know it.

Sooner or later that dream is dashed for 99.999% of us when puberty rears its ugly head. Take me, for instance. Among a plethora of other flaws, I abruptly stopped growing vertically in the fifth grade—5 feet 2 inches was all she wrote—finished, the end, short forevermore, one chromosome from being a dwarf. Still, thirty-six years later, friends and foe alike seem obliged to point out how "sho-o-o-rt" I am. Let's look at it in this light. We don't walk up to perfect strangers, much less friends, and declare, "You are so fat! How much do you weigh anyway, 250-275?" A fat person could sit on you and beat you about the head and ears then file a lawsuit for discrimination. Short people just keep smiling and saying apologetically, "I know, I know," then go on about the business, as tragic as it is, of being short. I say that it's time for the short people of the world to unite and take a stand against this injustice. Even if we have to use a stepladder, we must do it now, before it's too late.

Back to Miss America. Even at such a tender age, I caught on quickly to the hard truth that Miss Americas' aren't 5 feet 2 with big ears, fullback legs and a skillet butt. If it's not one of these flaws, then it could be the misfortune of having horse teeth, acne scars, a potato nose, crossed eyes, a pot belly, freckles the size of dimes, toothpick legs, knock knees, pigeon toes, etc., etc. The least little imperfection and you are out of the running. So, from that sad day forward, when you realize that you will never be Miss America, wear that coveted crown, and ride like a goddess in parades, it's time to just deal with it and move on to loftier goals.

As many things have since my tennis career began, it's become apparent to me that some women never completely got over it, so they crown themselves "Queen of the Whole Freakin' World." Or, God help us, they lucked up and won some two-bit crown after being bestowed the title of Watermelon or Tobacco Spitting Queen of Mize or Raleigh, Mississippi, respectively, or Miss Teen Princess of Tishomingo County back in 1980. In the back of her mind she is always thinking, "Nahhh-nahh-nah-booo-boo, I have a crown and you don't! I'm gorgeous, precious, and my feet don't stink."

Miss America will invariably arrive at the match "fashionably late." She will whip through the gates with the top of her convertible down. Amazingly, and to the nausea of all the V.G. s, not one hair will be blown asunder, for it is plastered with her special hurricane proof hair spray (available only at exclusive Miami salons). To her way of thinking, the tennis match is part of the physical fitness preliminary judging, and she must arrive in full regalia and makeup.

If you happen to be one of the contestants, I mean opponents, she will draw a bead on you like a hunter with the prey in his sight. You've got to hand it to her. She is an amicable creature, except bear in mind that her sole intention is that of whipping your homely ass and retaining her crown before she can break a

71

sweat during the judging, I mean the tennis match. She'll swiftly extend her right hand, as weighty as it is with diamonds, tennis bracelets, sculptured nails, etc., and, after taking a solitary deep breath, share more than you ever wanted or needed to know about her life. Imagine that you are on stage in Vicksburg competing for the coveted title of Miss Mississippi. As everyone knows, girls from Mississippi are always hard to reckon with in the Miss America pageant, but this chick is a real piece of work. Read the next sentence as fast as you can but with a Southern drawl. It may take a couple of tries to get it right, but it will be fun.

"HelloandwelcomeMynameisHeatherAnnI'llbeplayingnumbe ronesinglesIgraduatedfromOleMisswithadegreeintheartsMyhobbie saretennissunbathingandsnorkelingintheCarribeanItismydreamthat wewillhaveagoodmatchandnomatterwhowinswewillbeforeverfrien dswhenit'soverWhat'syournameandhowlonghaveyoubeencompeti ng!!" Whew!! After your head stops spinning and your ears quit ringing, she'll slow her monologue down a couple of notches, to that of a stereotypical G.R.I.T.S. (girl raised in the South).

"I jus' l-o-ove tha c-o-ompatishun, don't chew? Let's g-a-et stotted and s-e-e-e how we doo! My suv has bein jus' drrr-readful tha pas' few weeks. Please bayer with me 'cause I may not be much c-o-ompatishun. I've been on a dite the pas' few daze an I don't haf' enuff enajee to even swing the-iss racquet"

She weighs 105 pounds—tops—make-up, jewelry, saline bags, crown and all. You can't wait to get off the court and go to the Krystal to stuff your face. Why in the heck is she on a diet?

During the warm-up, after she finally stops chattering about her perfect life, there's not even a hint, weak and emaciated as she is, that her second serve travels with much topspin at approximately 95 m.p.h. She will bloop her practice serves over the net, giggle, snort, cover her mouth, coyly feign embarrassment and apologize for not giving you a good warm-up, until you are ready to puke. Then, after the spinning of the racquet to determine who serves first, she'll go to the bench, reach into her bag and pull out her imaginary crown. The spotlight is now on her as she takes the stage, I mean court, and prepares to knock the judges out of their seats. A metamorphosis of remarkable proportions is about to take place.

Pound for pound, "Miss America" can stroke the ball harder than most men of a comparable level. She is a turbo-charged, 105 pound dynamo with a deadly cross-court backhand. Nothing gets around or over her at the net. To top that off, she doesn't even sweat, not one shimmering drop on her glandless little, bronze body. When the match is over, the score will be more competitive than it should have been because you were dead set on making her sweat at least enough to smear her mascara. In your determination, you made some unbelievably gutsy shots that resulted in your salvaging a couple of games in each set. Amazingly, her makeup and hair will remain pageant perfect, and she will still reek of designer perfume to the bitter end. On the other side of the net, you will look like you just took a shower in your tennis clothes, but you won't smell like anything remotely close to designer perfume.

As you most assuredly will, when you do happen to meet a "Queen of the Whole Freakin' World" type on the court, my only suggestions are these: When you shake hands at the net, work up some crocodile tears and congratulate her on winning the physical fitness prelims, I mean match, and wish her luck at the state and national pageants, I mean tournaments. Reach across the net open-armed and give her a great, big, sweaty, stinky bear hug and a sloppy kiss on both cheeks. In the process, smear her makeup, if you can. Wink, smile sweetly, and walk away. She won't know what to think.

Karen C. Rasberry

The Man of Your Dreams Might Have Bad Breath...

After each match, there will usually be one or more of the team members who have fallen victim to Miss America, her mother, or the poster girls for emphysema. Whether the match was won or lost, it's time for celebration or consolation, whichever the case may be. When worse comes to worst, do what the V.G.'s do. Go drown your sorrows with your teammates at the Krystal drive thru. Grease is definitely salve for the deflated ego. There's nothing as comforting as stuffing your face with a dozen of those cheesy, square, steamy little delicacies and an oversized side order of greasy, salty French fries. We always order a bag of 48 cheeseburgers while a couple of the V.G. s hop out of the car and run next door to the 7-11 to pick up a brown-paper sack full of solace—melt-in-your mouth, deep, dark, cling-to-your-thighs, sinfully-rich CHOCOLATE.

Before we know it, our troubles and woes over losing are just fuzz off a tennis ball. We are laughing like hyenas and talking ninety-miles-an-hour about any and everything, not really paying attention until our favorite subject—SEX—pops up. At first mention of that magical word, all of the other conversations come to a screeching halt. You can hear a French fry drop as all eyes and ears turn to the V.G. that said the magic word.

That one, little, three-letter word sets off a chain reaction that can't be stopped. You never know how deep the conversation might go and where it might end. Someone pipes in and says she is going to give her husband a little treat when she gets home and another admits to doing so before she left for the match and another confesses who she would like to go a set or two with if she weren't morally convicted and loyal to her husband. The objects of our desire and fantasies are, of course, film stars, musicians or professional athletes who exist only in our dreams and on the movie screen or radio or who grace the covers of magazines. They are completely inaccessible, which makes it perfectly harmless to express what we would or could do to that said person if he miraculously happened to turn up on our doorstep bearing gifts. We all talk a big game, but if Mel, Brad, Harrison, Andre, Pete, or any one of our fantasy guys came to our door, we would probably faint, fall backwards, and lapse into a coma before we get to see what happens next.

Inevitably, the conversation turns to those poor souls outside of the car who are not morally convicted and are doing favors for everybody and his brother Believe me, everybody and his brother ain't from Hollywood. Some of you might call this gossip, but we consider it more like public service announcements that keep us abreast of local news. All the discussion about sex sometimes leads to a pertinent joke or two. One of the V.G.'s, who is a stereotypical Southern Belle with impeccable manners and would never utter anything distasteful, shocked us speechless one night when she told this joke on the way home from a tennis match:

Two highly respected local tennis playing women were having lunch at the club with a thrice-divorced woman who was reputed to have slept in more beds than George Washington. It just so happens that there was a big tennis tournament going on that weekend. There was this one guy from another town who had created some bad blood between himself and some of the local tennis boys. He was a pretty boy with a tanning bed tan who played in short shorts, sweat bands, gold chains, a $10,000 Rolex, and with a ghastly amount of chest hair spilling from the neck of his unbuttoned, monogrammed polo shirt. You know the type. Anyway, he went into the locker room to take a shower. While he was in there singing to the high Heavens, those tennis boys quietly took all his clothes and every last one of the towels, leaving him nothing but the keys to his Porsche. To get to his car, he would have to parade past the windows of the dining room, across a putting green, then streak 200 more yards to his car, which was parked near the tennis courts where the tournament was still *going on. The pretty boy jumped out of the shower and looked around for his bag, which was, by this time, in the dumpster behind the kitchen. To say the least, he was in a tight spot. He frantically searched the locker room for something, anything to cover his nakedness. The only thing he could find was a string mop used to clean the floors in the john. He thought to himself, "Should I cover my head with it so no one will recognize me or cover my genitals?" He had always been tickled with the size of that part of his anatomy, so he made the quick decision to conceal his identity instead of his manhood and make a run for it. He took the damp, putrid mop, placed it on his head wig style, pulled some of the strings down like bangs to cover his face and sprinted out of the locker room. Just about the time the women had finished their salads, one of them looked out the window, gasped and declared, "My goodness ga-rayshush, I do declare, there is a nekkid ma-an with a mop on his head!" After she observed his lower parts, she proclaimed with a sigh, "That ma-an is definitely not my husband." Appalled, with her mouth agape, the second woman exclaimed, "Why, my stars, my husband sure doesn't look like that." The third woman, with a twinkle in her eye and quiet lust in her voice, spoke up, "Why, ladies, I believe that ma-an isn't even a resident of this town and he certainly is not a member of this club."*

Since there is more than one blonde, bottle or otherwise, in the group, it took a moment for the punch line to sink in. When it did, hysterical laughter erupted as Krystal burgers and French fries spewed all over the S.U. V we were riding in. The V.G. that told the joke was rather delighted that she had caused such a hullabaloo, but nevertheless, begged us not to ever tell her mother, her husband, or her preacher that she had told such an off-color joke. Since she was new to the team and we had doubts about her eagerness to become one of us, that was the pivotal moment when she first became a true V.G.

What a fine time V.G. s have when we lose a tennis match. After years of experience, we have discovered that losing is sometimes just as much . fun as winning because we have a legitimate excuse to do whatever it takes to get out of the doldrums. Don't start losing intentionally because winning is still the preferred outcome. We would always much rather be in the "W" club than the "L" club for the season, but winning in the local competition and advancing to district play, even with all its perks, is highly overrated. Compare winning to finally having the opportunity to fulfill your fantasies with Mel Gibson, Brad Pitt, or whoever it is that melts your candle, only to discover that his breath would gag a buzzard, he doesn't wear deodorant and has hair sprouting from his ears. If you keep this comparison in mind, your emotions about winning and losing should always stay on an even keel.

I guess what I have been trying to say with all this rambling is that you should never, ever underrate your opponent and the valuable lessons to be learned from losing or overestimate your own abilities and the virtues of winning. Good tennis players come in all shapes, sizes, and ages. Unfortunately, there is no magic rule-of-thumb to determine which ones those might be until you have actually been across the net from them. The longer you play the game and the more opponents you encounter, the more astute you will become at recognizing them before play begins.

Not wanting to come across as being politically incorrect or mean spirited, I intentionally have not elaborated on a few stereotypes who have the potential to whip your oblivious fanny. Do not discount and always keep a suspicious eye on: Women with spiked hair who compliment your legs during the warm-up, really obese women who convey the impression that they are physically incapable or too generously proportioned to run down the best shot you've got, and women who are wearing any type of brace, bandage or orthopedic device. On any given day, they can leave you on the bench crying in your Gatorade.

Forgive me. I almost left one out. Beware, if you are warming up with a woman who says she is just back into the game after having a hysterectomy; you might require one yourself when the match is over.

After many years in the real estate business, I have found that once a house gets to be about fifty years old, the pipes and drains are bound to start springing leaks and clogging up. The buyer has the option of patching and calling Roto-Rooter once a month or replacing the whole shebang. There is a strong parallel between fifty-year-old women and fifty-year-old houses; except with women, you can't replace the plumbing, so you have it all removed. A house with no plumbing is better than having no house at all. It has been strongly suggested to me by my husband that it might be just what I need to cure everything that ails me (the list is lengthy). Women without uteri (or is it uteruses?) seem to feel much better than the rest of the poor souls who are still dealing with all the hormonal surges. They simply receive hormone replacement therapy and never have to be bothered with mood swings, hot flashes, P.M.S. or murderous thoughts again.

By the way, do you know the difference between a woman with P.M.S. and an axe murderer? Women with P.M.S. prefer to use their bare hands. This isn't a medically proven, scientific fact, but in talking with them, 100% say they feel as if they have obtained a new lease on life and are ready to conquer the world, which includes you. Two of the V.G. s recently had all their plumbing removed and are playing the best tennis of their lives. One of them was having some difficulty getting her sex drive back to where it was pre-hysterectomy. Last week she was happy to report that she had just visited the wisest hormone doctor in these parts. He promised her that in no time at all she would be down at the fire station looking for somebody to "please put her fire out." After playing them and a few other women who were post-op by a few weeks, I say without reservation, "Sharpen up your scalpel and sign me up Doc, I'm ready!!"

Karen C. Rasberry

The Joys of Multiple Partners...

Unlike sex, tennis is an activity in life where you can have multiple partners and not be considered promiscuous. On more than one occasion, some of the V.G.'s have been referred to as "tennis whores" because of our tendency to play with anybody, anytime, anywhere. We don't take offense to this label at all. To be candid, I must confess that I have been with as many as four different men in one afternoon. We are rather conceited over our popularity and ability to scrape up a tennis match with the guys in a matter of minutes.

We truly enjoy one another's company and playing together during the regular women's and combo seasons, but it is mixed doubles that we enjoy the most. It provides a change of pace in the type of game we play and offers a welcome change of scenery. In mixed doubles there's less pressure to win, less bickering, more nonsense, and more opportunity to improve your level of play. You may just love and crave chocolate chip ice cream; but if you eat it every day for a few months, you eventually get sick at the sight of it. That's what mixed doubles is all about—a little taste of something different. The more flavors you try, the better it gets.

It took my husband years to become complacent about the mixed doubles thing, but once he finally figured out that I was just "using" those men to fulfill a need that he wasn't willing or able to provide, he decided life is too short to worry about losing me to my mixed doubles partner. Husbands are easy to come by, but finding a compatible mixed doubles partner is a rare and precious thing.

One early Saturday morning, after trying to contact one of my regular mixed doubles partners for days, I strolled up to the courts and caught him red-handed playing with a woman I had never seen before.

I yelled through the fence, "There you are, you little playboy, I have caught you cheating on me again!!"

Shameless, he quipped back, "Oh, come on darling, you know how much I love you!!"

Faking tears now, he pleads in a desperate tone of voice, "Please, please let me make it up to you."

After all the bantering through the fence, the strange woman was ready to pick up her bag and bolt from the court. It wasn't until their opponents burst out laughing that she realized we were just having a little harmless fun at her expense. She didn't know that he is notorious for being the biggest bag of wind and shameless flirt in the whole state of Mississippi. Although he is very happily married to an understanding woman, he just loves women, all women, and they all love him. He has a compliment for each and every one he meets. It doesn't matter if her body shows that she has beaten a path through one too many "all-you-can-eat" buffets or that her face could make a freight train take a dirt road, he will make her feel like she's the most gorgeous woman alive. Most of the time he is so full of himself, you never know when he's telling the truth or shooting the bull. Nonetheless, I fall for his lines every time and feel like Meg Ryan when I am in his presence. He can even make losing a match rewarding when he says, "Thank you for just being you."

Partners like him are what makes mixed doubles so appealing. Just as the net divides the court, there is an imaginary line drawn between mixed doubles partners that strictly prohibits hanky-panky and fooling around. That line has been rumored to get a little blurry and hard to distinguish at times, but we V.G. s have made it a policy to never cross it. We love the game too much to mess up a good mixed doubles team (and a marriage) by crossing that invisible barrier.

We admire and depend on our mixed doubles partners not just on the court but off it as well. One day last summer I left work to go to lunch and found one of the tires on my Jeep flatter than a flitter. Although it wasn't beyond my capabilities, I wasn't about to jack up a car in nine-hundred-degree heat in the middle of a parking lot that sits alongside the busiest street in town. It never crossed my mind to call my husband. It was my long-time mixed doubles partner that got the call to come to my rescue. Why? Because he operates a tire store and I knew he would send somebody to rescue his favorite female partner.

When I broke into hives and began suffering from marked shortness of breath after taking an antibiotic, I didn't share with my husband that I was about thirty seconds from being his dearly departed wife. It was my sometime partner, the pharmacist, who, over the phone, saved my life by telling me not to panic and to take some Benedryl S.T.A.T.

A while back, my daughter was being manipulated and sweet-talked by a much older, baggy-breeched, orange-haired musician. He had her believing that he was the next big thing and was about to shoot up the charts on a major label. What's a mother supposed to do in such a helpless situation? Well, I called up one of my mixed doubles partners who just so happens to be an attorney-at-law with two daughters of his own. His first response was strictly a paternal one.

"Well, I can help you kill the little turd if you want me to."

His knowledge of the law and common sense prevailed as he helped me decide what to do. With many thanks to my lawyer tennis buddy, I haven't seen the little orange-haired weasel in quite a while. If I never see him again, it will be too soon.

And then there is this one guy I play with who knew me way back when we were in high school before time, gravity and life got a hold of us. When I am on the court with him, although he is now a grandfather of two, time has stood still. In my eyes, he is still the star running back of our 1970 conference winning football team. With good reason, he's still a little cocky (you know you are) and has an air about him that girls loved thirty years ago and still do to this day. Although he has never said so, I would like to believe that he still sees me as that perky little cheerleader who once had nice, firm legs free from cellulite and varicose veins and could jump higher, cartwheel, and scream louder than any of the other girls on the squad. One thing I do know is that the shared remembrance of what we once were in our youth inspires us to play out of minds when we are together on the court. Since both of us are vertically challenged, but remain undaunted by our towering opponents, his wife and daughter have proclaimed us the "Mighty Mites."

Like the Mayflower Madam, my little black book of partners could go on and on, so I will spare you the juicy details. But, I must tell you about one last partner. Life dealt him a sucker punch in the gut about ten years ago when his teenage daughter was paralyzed in an auto accident. Now a married woman with a college degree, she is a survivor and a fighter who is determined to knock down the obstacles in her path. I can only imagine what the whole family has been through since the accident. Love, faith, hope, and prayer have held them together. This guy never ceases to amaze me because he never seems to be down or depressed. He always keeps on the sunny side of life when dwelling on the dark side would be the easy way out. In my heart, I know that tennis is one of the things that has helped him maintain his buoyant outlook and zest for life.

If you are ever fortunate enough to play tennis with him you are going to laugh at yourself. You are going to have a superior time. You are going to be called a "meat head" or an "imbecile." You will learn to do high fives with the knuckles of your fist. You are going to forget about the petty little problems that seemed so mountainous before you started playing. And, chances are, you are going to beat the "shidookie" out of your opponents. Thanks, "meat head," for helping me (literally and figuratively) keep my eye on the ball.

To all the wives of the men that I have played tennis with, thanks for sharing and trusting me. And to the men who have been burdened with having me as their partner, you are the brothers I never had, my friends, and my taste of something different. If I am around when it happens, at your funerals, to raise some eyebrows, rest assured that I'll blubber, wail, and carry on to beat the band as if we were once lovers instead of old tennis partners. And, I'll even slip a fresh can of balls into your casket just in case they don't have any in Heaven.

The Do's and Don'ts of Mixed Doubles...

As I promised earlier in this book, we will discuss in some detail the dos and don'ts of mixed doubles. The first rule in mixed doubles is to never, ever, unless he is the last able-bodied man left on the face of the Earth, play doubles with your spouse. It goes against the rules of God and nature and can turn very ugly. Men and women were meant to abide together and produce offspring. The Bible says, "Be fruitful and multiply the Earth." Nowhere does it say, "Be stupid and play tennis together." Spousal mixed doubles is a fruitless endeavor that has been known to lead to world class cuss-outs, and in the worst of cases, assault and battery with a stringed weapon followed by divorce court.

Imagine this scenario. Phyllis and Phil have been blissfully married for twelve years when they decide to play mixed doubles together. Things don't go so smoothly as they had planned. Their marriage has weathered storm after storm, but it can't weather losing three tennis matches in a row. They wind up in divorce court. The judge inquires as to why they are seeking a divorce.

The husband responds, "Your honor, my wife has concrete feet."

The judge looks down at her feet and notices that she is sporting a rather nice pair of Brighton loafers. He responds, "Her feet look perfectly normal to me. Could you elaborate a little more as to the meaning of "concrete feet"?

The husband replies, "Sir, her feet aren't literally made of concrete. I simply meant that she won't move her feet on the tennis court when I tell her to go for a ball."

The judge inquires, "And you think that is grounds for a divorce?"

"Your honor, she not only won't move her feet, but she tattooed me with her tennis racquet squarely on the top of my head after I subtly suggested that she might try a little harder to go for a ball. Sir, she physically assaulted me and humiliated me in front of our opponents and my teammates. As you can see, I don't have much hair up there so the kids now try to play tic-tac-toe on my head with a magic marker. To add to my pain and humiliation, the tennis pro called the police, and they almost took me to jail for disturbing the peace. Thankfully, they removed the handcuffs and put away their pistols after I explained to them that we were just having a little, marital disagreement and that it would never, ever happen again."

The judge responds, "You said you quietly asked your wife to try to do better when you were playing a tennis match together. If so, then why were the police called to the scene?"

Suddenly and without warning, the wife with the alleged concrete feet jumps like a scalded cat from her chair and shrieks at the top of her lungs, "He yelled at me, your honor, and called me names I wouldn't call my worst enemy. He deserved to have his brainless head branded, and I'd do it again right now if I had a tennis racquet because he's a selfish, lying, beer-gutted, pitiful excuse for a tennis player, and I absolutely refuse to be married to such a low-life piece of humanity for another second. On top of that, our four-year-old has a better serve than he does, and I'm sick to death of washing his dirty, stinking socks!!"

Need I say more about the folly of spousal mixed doubles?

In my many years of tennis playing, I have known only one couple that has managed to play mixed doubles and maintain a happy union. I'm proud to say that the female half of that team is one of the esteemed V.G.s. However, maintaining a happy marriage and a doubles partnership requires unlimited patience, uncommon understanding and the occasional administering of an attitude adjustment. All it takes is a summons with her index finger and a dismayed look. With one hand on her hip and the other clenching her racquet by her side, she huddles coolly and quietly with her mate on the baseline. Presto! Change-o! Just like magic, he emerges from his adjustment a new and improved man. She has never divulged to anyone exactly what she whispers in his ear. This V.G. is one smart cupcake, smart enough that the state of Mississippi issued her a license to dispense controlled substances. Knowing her and her uncanny ability to use reverse psychology, I suspect it has something to do with his love life or the possibility that he will be denied one for the rest of his natural born virile days if he doesn't straighten up and quit acting like an idiot. Although V.G.'s don't advocate man and wife mixed doubles, it is acceptable in extremely rare cases.

Now that you know the #1 rule and the primary secret to happiness in mixed doubles, we can move on to the equally important rule #2. It is a simple rule. Always tell your husband or significant other the truth about the man you are spending so much of your time with. If you tell him your partner is sixty-eight-years-old, deaf in both ears, had his testicles shot off in Korea, wears his dead uncle's toupee, and lives in and drives a '78 Lincoln Town Car, he will eventually become suspicious and start seeking the truth. When he finds out that your partner is, in fact, a single, thirty-one-year old bodybuilder who once flew with the Blue Angels and now owns his own airline, not to mention the fact that he rides a Harley Davidson and wears black leather while doing so, the proverbial crap is going to hit the fan and splatter all over you. If you don't come clean the first time he asks, at least tell the truth the second time before it is forevermore too late. If you get busted for stretching the truth (outright lying), even if you thought it was in his own best interest not to know the truth, he'll never let you leave the house alone for as long as you live. Or worse yet, he'll come watch you every time you practice or play. Then, neither one of you will be getting any enjoyment out of life.

Even if you follow these first two rules to the letter, it doesn't necessarily mean that everything will be smooth sailing at your house. Here are a few more simple guidelines to achieve a successful mixed doubles partnership. If your mixed doubles partner doesn't fall within these parameters, you could still find yourself in hot water on the home front.

1. Your partner must be old enough to be your grandfather or

2. You must be old enough to be his grandmother or
3. He can be your husband's best friend from birth (and impotent) or
4. The preacher who baptized you (if you are a Baptist) or
5. Your husband's father or your own father or
6. Your own son or
7. Your own grandson or
8. Your blood brother (not step) or
9. If your husband is not very rich, gorgeous, influential, sexy, etc, then
10. Your partner must be flat broke, have a "comb over" hairdo, be morbidly obese, have a psycho wife who would chop off your fingers if you ever touched him, six children under the age of five, and they all must live in government housing with his mother-in-law or
11. Your gynecologist (he's seen more of you than he ever wanted to) or
12. George Clooney (highly improbable but merely smelling his sweat would be worth getting a divorce) or
13. Gay (flaming)

Also, your mixed partner cannot be a priest, wear gold chains or wear "wife beaters," shorts so short that it makes you nauseous, have visible tattoos, oversized feet or drive a Porsche.

Since I have already won my husband's trust after twenty-eight years of being faithful and true, none of my mixed doubles partners currently fall within these guidelines. In other words, I am so old and have been married long enough to be exempt from any and all restrictions. These guidelines are for you younger, more attractive women who are just beginning to play the game with a partner of the opposite sex. I have never played tennis with my grandson or brother (don't have any), my father-in-law (he's deceased), my own father (he's 84), George Clooney (a girl can dream), or a gay man, that I'm aware of.

There was this one reasonably handsome guy a few years back who seemed a little "iffy." When the oft debated subject of his sexual preference came up in the car on the way to a tennis match, a former V.G. wanna-be (single at the time) nonchalantly informed us that she had recently done some private investigative work under cover of darkness on the back nine in a golf cart while wearing nothing but her tennis shoes and a smile. Dead silence filled the car as our imaginations ran amuck at the thought of such a scenario. A million questions raced through our minds when someone finally cut the silence with that all-important one:

"Well, is he gay or is he not, and why haven't you said something already?"

Like a prisoner being interrogated for conspiracy to commit murder, she spilled her guts. "He did come up a little "short," if you know what I mean, but the way he kissed and the rest of his body actually made up for the deficit. If he's gay, then I'm Mother Teresa. The reason I haven't said anything before now is that I didn't want the whole free world to know until the time was right. I kind of like knowing a secret that everybody else wants to know."

Someone pleaded for the driver to turn up the air conditioning as the rest of us heaved a sigh of liberation (or disappointment), "Well, we sure are relieved that you solved that lingering question." And, that was the last word that any of us ever uttered about him and his sexual preferences. It was time to move on to the next unsolved mystery. We had to find another fish to fry.

Of all the men I haven't played tennis with yet, I think it would be absolutely the best of both worlds to have a gay man as a tennis partner. Just think of all the enjoyable things you could do together, and your husband wouldn't give it a second thought. Your husband would be free to fish, play golf, watch wrestling or NASCAR, piddle around the yard, or whatever he likes with complete trust and confidence that you will come home to him when the match is over.

I can just picture it now. As I arrive at the match, he greets me with a hug and a kiss for both cheeks.

"Umm wah! O-o-o-h, mah, gahd! You look so sexy in that skirt!! Is it 100% or stretchy cotton? It makes your buns look s-o-o good. Don't lie to me. Does my outfit make my thighs look firm? Is this color O.K. on me? You know how lavender tends to wash me out."

I assure him, "Don't be so paranoid, you look fine and firm all over."

He replies with a flick of his wrist, "Oh, girl, I've gained right around the middle. I'm gonna' just have to start step aerobic classes again."

During the match you can pat him on the booty after he makes a nice shot, and nobody will give it a second thought except that maybe he's not gay after all. When the match is over, he'll apologize repeatedly for his untidy appearance and declare that he is sweating like a June bride in a feather bed and is in immediate need of a shower and a massage.

Afterwards, you can escape for a cappuccino in a bookstore coffee shop and give each other tips on decorating and exchange beauty secrets. He can go shopping with you and help you pick out the perfect tennis dress by telling you exactly which styles and colors are "you" and which ones are "not." He will listen attentively while you pour out your heart about how your husband doesn't understand you and that he never talks to you or pays you any attention unless he wants something. Then he will tell you what a lucky man your husband is to have such a wonderful, attractive, caring woman who plays tennis solely to keep herself in shape for him. What he says will be straight from the heart and not wrapped around some macho Romeo underhanded motive. The beauty of the whole thing is that he will not be sexually attracted to you and won't pose a threat to your husband in any way, shape or form. Voila!! The perfect man!!

My fantasy of having a gay man as a tennis partner as well as a companion has almost inspired me to run a personal ad in the local newspapers and on the internet. It would read something like this: Wanted. Gay man, age 30-55, to pal around with straight, married female. Must be a non-fisherman, able to play tennis competitively, enjoy shopping, conversation, music, books, sunbathing, possess a good sense of humor and be financially independent. Call 101-555-1234 anytime day or night.

This chapter may well be the most important one of all, so read it twice if you didn't understand it the first time. Mixed doubles can be a little precarious at times, so you must always remain diligent in finding the right partner. With no offense to the dearly beloved V.G. s, if I had the choice of playing regular women's doubles or mixed, I'd have to choose playing with the guys because they never get moody with you, rarely let the "green eyed monster" show up at a match; and they never, ever worry about what they are wearing or how their hair looks, mainly because many of them don't have hair anyway.

You Might Be Addicted to Tennis if...

Have you ever, after playing fifteen sets of tennis in one weekend, decided that maybe you ought to cut back a smidgeon on your quest for tennis perfection? After all, we are never going to make it to the French Open, or for that matter, the national championships. Wouldn't it be nice to get to know the spouse and the kids again? Your daughter is graduating from high school next year and you thought she was in the ninth grade. The last time you took your wife out to dinner was two years ago. You thought the #3 at McDonald's with a view of the playground was a nice gesture, but she is pestering you to give her "more."

Or, have you ever attempted to get out of bed on Monday morning after a big tournament, and your back just wouldn't cooperate? Does it feel like a wet towel that has been twisted and twisted into a tight braid similar to a pretzel? Does your elbow ever lock up with excruciating pain as you reach to turn off the alarm clock? When you try to straighten your legs, does the area behind your kneecaps feel like there is gravel grinding around in there? You think to yourself—is that normal, or does everyone have these problems? No. Everyone does not have these problems, unless they once played professional sports or, in our case, are addicted to adult league tennis.

It's true that everyone who plays tennis is not addicted to the game. Some recreational players are able to enjoy the game in moderation for a number of years without ever showing signs of addiction. Others start out playing like a fiend then burn themselves out like a shooting star within a few months. The addicts (like the volley girls and many others I know) are, after many years, countless injuries, and major obstacles, still just as whacked out as they were that first time they got high on tennis.

From what I've read on the subject, most drug addicts know when they are addicted but deny there is a real problem until someone intervenes. I suppose it's the same way with tennis players. We know we've got a problem, but there are so many, much more dreadful things to be addicted to, so we simply ignore the signs. If the game does begin to interfere with your ability to hold a job, keep your marriage together, or lands you in the slammer, then it's just about time to get some help.

If you can relate to four of the following "ifs," you might be addicted to tennis. If you say yes to five of these "ifs," you are playing with frayed strings. If you say yes to six or more, seeking help for your addiction is advisable, but you are a poor candidate for rehabilitation.

You might be addicted to tennis if:

You are reading this book.

Your cat or daughter is named Steffi or your dog or son's name is Andre.

The license plate on your car reads ILUV10S, 10SNE1, N210S, 40LUV, or 10SFREK,

You go shopping for a dress to wear to your aunt's funeral and decide that she would want you to have a new tennis dress instead of that depressing black frock you almost bought. She always did like you the best and won't care if you wear a flour sack to bid her farewell.

You have ever played tennis on Sunday morning, in the sleet, during a tornado warning, Christmas Eve, New Year's Day, your baby's due date, or your wedding day.

Your neighbors shake their heads in disbelief every time you squeal out of your driveway wearing a visor.

Your closet smells like a tribe of goat herders resides in it because there are nineteen pairs of worn out tennis shoes hidden away in there.

Your key chain, desk, purse, luggage, office wall, wrist or neck has anything pertaining to tennis hanging on it.

Your second-grader tells her teacher that "Mommy played tennis **again** and Daddy was mad" when asked why she didn't do her homework the night before.

You have a big match at 6:00 P.M. but tell your big shot client that you can't meet with him because it's your 10th anniversary—even though you filed divorce papers last week.

You play tennis nine days after having your gallbladder removed or two weeks after having a complete hysterectomy.

The sound and then the aroma of opening a new can of balls gives you a big rush.

Four times a year, during Wimbledon, the French Open, the Australian Open, and the U.S. Open, your family unplugs the T.V. and tells you it was struck by lightening again. (They would rather look at the four walls or play Old Maids than listen to you say, "My God, did you see that point!!? That was so awesome!"

You have a cast on your tennis arm but quickly learn to play with your other arm.

You spend $450.00 on a new racquet, outfit and shoes in Minneapolis during the dead of winter on a business trip after discovering that your hotel has an indoor tennis court and a teaching pro who offers lessons at $50.00 per hour.

You make it to your 11:00 A.M. lesson after visiting your husband in ICU at 10:00 A.M. (Hey, they only let you stay 20 minutes and the nurses have your cell phone number if he codes.)

You know your USTA number by heart but can't remember your Social Security number.

You remember your wins-losses record for the past five years.

You have more than six outdated racquets in the storage closet that you just can't bear to part with.

You have enough old tennis balls lying around that if they were recycled could put new tires on every tractor in Texas.

The doctor injects your elbow with cortisone in the morning (which hurts like a gunshot wound) and you go out and play that afternoon after he emphatically told you to lay off a couple of weeks or it would never heal.

When you play tennis you have so many braces and wraps on your limbs that you resemble an Egyptian mummy.

Your child has a temp of 103 degrees, the commode just overflowed, and the roast in the oven has burst into flames. It's 6:30 and your match is at 7:00. Your spouse just walked through the door with a look that could kill. What would you do?:

- A. Call your captain and say you can't make it.
- B. Call the doctor.
- C. Call the plumber.
- D. Dial 911.
- E. Kiss your spouse on the cheek and say you're late for the match as you are running out the door.

If you are truly addicted to tennis the answer is E. There's no need to call your captain because none of these excuses are serious enough. Your spouse is perfectly capable of dialing the doctor, the plumber, and 911.

Good luck, God bless, and remember that you are not alone.

Road Trip—September 2001

It's has already been determined that the V.G. s absolutely love road trips. It is most often the case, but road trips don't necessarily have to be centered around tennis. Sometimes it's more fun to hit the open highway with no particular itinerary in mind. Just load up half of everything we own, take off and see what happens. Incommunicado. That is exactly what we had in mind last September when four of us planned an impromptu getaway to Orange Beach, Alabama, just a stones' throw from the Florida line.

We were all set. Miraculously, the kids were healthy, happy, and all taken care of. None of them were presently suffering from snotty noses, diarrhea, or vomiting. The husbands were more agreeable than normal about our departure due to all the favors that had been copiously heaped upon their masculinity. One V.G. lamented that she had to do some serious acrobatics with her husband to get him to leave her alone long enough to pack her bags.

"No joke, to go on this trip, I would have stood on my head naked, twirled plates on the soles of my feet, and whistled "Dixie" all at the same time if it would make him happy." We all agreed that was a reasonable price to pay for a couple of days' R & R.

By 8:30 a.m. on Tuesday, September 11, our plans had been confirmed. We were to launch our mission with military skill at exactly 0700 hours on September 13. Within the hour everything around us changed forever. Immediately, the news media started comparing the attacks on the World Trade Center to Pearl Harbor.

I'm not old enough to remember Pearl Harbor, but my daddy was there on a ship December 7, 1941. He survived and went on to fight other battles from the Pacific to the Atlantic. His life and our country turned on that infamous day. The horror of it all has filtered through him to me in ways that are hard to explain. As a result, even though I wasn't born until fourteen years later, sometimes I feel that part of me was there, too. Over the past sixty-one years, my daddy has never spoken much about how he felt that day. His lack of verbal communication on the subject has served as a constant reminder of how life changing it really was.

Then, although I was only eight, there is another day I remember vividly. It changed the course of American history. If you ever visit Arlington Cemetery, you will see that Americans still mourn the loss of John Fitzgerald Kennedy just as helplessly as they did in the fall of 1963. It is an open wound on the soul of America that will never heal. For those who can remember, it was the day that our postwar ideals and the dreams of "Camelot" were shattered. People my age and older are the ones who tend to gaze into the eternal flame a little longer, reflect more deeply, still try to comprehend how it happened, and wonder how things might have been if he had lived.

Shock. Anger. Disbelief. Fear. All these words can't adequately convey the emotions the whole country felt on September 11, 2001. I'm censoring the words here, but my thoughts were along the lines of, "Those filthy, under slung, towel-headed cowards! Who do they think they are, and what kind of god do they serve?" If those murdering hijackers could contact Osama Bin Laden from where they are right now, they would, no doubt, be calling him a low down, lying, sack of camel dung for convincing them to martyr themselves in the name of a false god. This is strictly from a flawed, human perspective, but I am confident that God will see to it that they get to enjoy crashing airplanes into the gates of Hell 24-7 from here to eternity. Just before impact, they will be forced to look into the eyes of the innocent children, women, and men that they murdered. They will struggle desperately to say, "I'm sorry," but the words will never come.

So, what do we do now? We can hide in fear for the rest of our lives or go about the business of living, and in doing so, prove to them that they will never take away our freedom?

On September 13, just as we had planned, at three minutes past 0700 hours, four Southern-American girls took the high road. There was nothing we could do but pray for our country, ourselves, and the families of the brave ones who had lost their lives. With the Greatest Hits of the 1969 in the C.D. player as our mantra and an American flag defiantly flapping from the rear window, we set our inner compasses toward the Gulf of Mexico. The early morning sun winked in and out of the trees and glistened on the dewy grass. We were young and the days until school began again were more than we could count. We didn't have a worry in the world until the moment was spoiled by the maddening, ring, ring, ring of a cell phone. Wouldn't you just know it? It was a husband faking distress. We only heard the captive end of the conversation. It went something like this.

"Helloooo......What!?......Good Lord a mighty! You felt fine this morning when I left......Why didn't you say something?......So, it's your left arm?......Is it like a strained kind of hurt or is it a heart attack kind of hurt?......Why aren't you sure?......201 over 105!!!......If the EKG is O.K. and your blood pressure goes down, is he going to let you go back to work?......That's good. They have medicine for that. I'm sure you'll be fine. Have the doctor call me if you need me, and don't forget to pick up your child at 2:45......I love you......By the way, did you pay your life insurance premium this month?...Gotta go now...Yes, I'll call...See you Sunday......Of course we won't go to the Flora-Bama......Bye. Kiss, Kiss."

"What was all that about? Do we need to turn around and go see about him?"

"Ohhh, Hell! There's not a blasted thing wrong with him! He's healthier than a horse. He's just wants to ruin my weekend and make me feel guilty. He does this every single time I go out of town. Chest pains, high blood pressure, nausea. He's got to come up with a new set of symptoms if he expects me to stay my ass at home all the time rattling them pots and pans."

Forget the terrorists and the heart attacks! Full speed ahead! Heart attack or no heart attack, terrorists or not, it was the end of summer, and we still owned the right to squeeze the last little bit of enjoyment from it. Before we knew it, we were transformed into giggling, carefree, not-so-innocent teenagers wearing cut-off blue jeans, flip flops and some long-forgotten boyfriend's class ring. As we breathed in the salty air of Mobile Bay, we tried our best to overlook the fact that we had already crossed that great divide which forever separated us from the carefree summer days of our youth.

We weren't seventeen anymore, but we had all the trappings—bikinis, Coppertone suntan lotion, the original white potion with that smell that gives me chill bumps; and we had the music that would tie our memories up into a sweet little bundle. We also had three whole days of glorious freedom ahead of us. Our mission—to enjoy ourselves as much as possible under the circumstances, to fight the enemy the only way we knew how by flying "Old Glory" and by waving and honking at every car we passed as a sign of unity.

Life's a Parade at the Beach...

If you can tell me of another place on this earth, other than the beach, that can make your troubles seem small, allows you to feel at complete peace with yourself and improves your whole outlook on life, please tell me where it is, because I'm packing my bags after I finish this sentence.

Earlier in this book I mentioned that what the V.G. s have in common is that we are all married with children. That statement must be amended here and now. Each one of us also loves the beach in a fanatical way. We all have a place that we consider "home"—not the place where we physically abide, but that place where our hearts yearn to be. For the V.G. s, it's near the shore, where the air, sand, and saltwater have a way of getting into the blood. To quote the sentiments of the most notorious beach bum of them all, Jimmy Buffett claims that, "It cleans me out, then I can go on."

There is nothing so soothing to the soul as the symphony of the waves, salty mist on the face, sand twixt and between every crevice of your body, watching seagulls as they dive and float on thick, salty breezes in the morning sun. There is something primal or even innate that beckons us year after year. We migrate to the ocean instinctively with our young in tow, just as birds gather their flocks and fly south for the winter.

A summer's day at the beach is an exhibition of human beings in various stages and ages of this journey we call life. Often, it is impossible to focus on the bestseller I am trying to read, when the parade that passes in front of me is more spellbinding than any novel ever written.

Shiny, bronze teenage girls promenade by in packs with brightly colored triangles strategically placed over dangerous curves. They are the ones that make us feel antique, as obsolete as a Ford Fairlane in a showroom full of sexy, Mustang convertibles. Oh, to be that age again, unscathed by gravity, oblivious to time or worry, and completely giddy that the blonde-haired boy with the surfboard might be looking my way.

Young parents watch sun-kissed toddlers play chase with the surf. They build sand castles with plastic shovels and take naps under festive umbrellas that dot the shore. I have to resist walking over to them with a warning to seize the day and to keep the moment deep in their hearts. They have to realize that they are making precious, fleeting memories that cannot be recreated the "next time." Watching them makes me long desperately for those days when I showed my children the wonders of the beach for the first time. It is my prayer that I can carry on the tradition with my unborn grandchildren.

I am amused and heartened by silver haired retirees with copper pot bellies strolling along with their matronly spouses. Modestly attired for the beach, they sport awning-like straw hats to shield them from the sun. They seldom hold hands, but I sense a lasting commitment and a deep contentment between them that comes only by weathering life's storms together. As they meander by, it becomes a game of sorts to guess what profession they were in before they retired. Perhaps they were bankers, stockbrokers, nurses, truckers, or teachers, who lived modestly, invested wisely, and fulfilled their dream of retiring to the coast. Some of them appear athletic enough. Perhaps they play tennis and were once club champion. Maybe they are the reigning club champion or are ranked #1 in their age category for an entire state. You just never know about people (Re: They Will Beat You Every Time). In the blink of an eye, the same span of time that it took my toddlers to spring from my arms and dart joyously through the sand to the sea, I will become one of them.

In the parade are joggers and should-be joggers, lovers, loners, and searchers of themselves. Sedated by the waves and the sun, I place my open book face down on the beach towel beside me, pull down my visor, and drift in and out of consciousness with each crash and wane of the waves.

When we arrived at our destination on September 13, 2001, everything was eerily quiet for that time of the year. Despite one of the deepest, blue skies that we had ever seen, everything was closed up and battened down as if a category 4 hurricane was churning full tilt toward land. The Flora-Bama Lounge, a world-renowned juke joint that straddles the Alabama-Florida line, was open for business, but even the mood there was respectfully downcast. Their billboard, which generally tempts beachgoers with "Live Music, Cold Beer and Wet T-shirt Contest Tonight," had been toned down. It patriotically read, "God Bless America."

Even the waves seemed to break at half-mast in reply to the tragedy that had befallen our country. We optimistically hauled all our stuff to the beach, carefully greased every inch of our bodies with coconut suntan oil, arranged our chairs, towels, magazines, music box, and munchies so that we wouldn't have to move a finger or at the most, a hand, for the rest of the afternoon. "Lissez les bon temps rouler." As much as we wanted to "let the good times roll," they wouldn't budge an inch. It was impossible to block out the images of airplanes crashing into buildings, towers collapsing, and the absolute terror on the faces of those who ran for their lives. We called our children and our husbands on our cell phones just to see if they were all right. A bright note was that, when he was released by his doctor, the "heart attack" husband decided to enjoy a round of golf instead of going back to work. What did we ever do without cell phones, especially during times of national crisis?

Then we said in unison, "Do you think we need to get back inside the condo and catch the news? Something else could be happening, and we wouldn't even know it. It just ain't right for us to be out here. Nobody else is."

Then we remembered that we were only a few miles from the Pensacola Naval Air Station. What if a band of terrorists was lying in wait ready to blow the whole area to smithereens? If we were terrorists, that's definitely where we'd strike. Yeah, we'd destroy the home of the Blue Angels along with every blue and yellow F/A-18 Hornet that symbolizes all that is brave and good about America, then we'd proceed west, knocking down the sugar white sand castles and memories of thousands of families. When

101

we reached Mobile Bay, we'd sink the U.S.S. Alabama, plant mines under the bay bridge, and as a grand finale, explode a tanker truck in the Bankhead Tunnel. God, I hope that no terrorists read this and get some big ideas.

We were horrified that our simple, peace loving minds could even formulate such a sinister chain of events. We attributed our disturbing thoughts to the fact that it had really happened in New York City. If it happened there, then it could most certainly happen here in the heart of one of the premier playgrounds of the Southeast. Paranoia had definitely set in. Panic was just a few steps behind.

The endless drone of what we hoped were surveillance airplanes flying back and forth along the horizon forced us to finally let it all sink in. We realized that things would never be the same as they were before at the beach, at home or anywhere else. From September 11th forward, we would always be looking cautiously over our shoulders, never board another airplane without checking out the faces of our fellow passengers, or maybe we'd never be brave enough to fly again. An apprehensive feeling would shadow our every move. There was no more imagining how frightened and helpless our parents felt on December 7, 1941. It was Pearl Harbor all over again. Except this time, we and our children had witnessed it over and over in living color in the comfort of our living rooms.

Of the four of us who made the trip to the beach that weekend, only one had ever been to New York City. Her trip was over twenty years before, and the memory of it was spotty and had gray areas that she couldn't fill in. New York City, for me, had always been one of those places I'd love to visit just for the sake of saying I had been there. Women like me had no business reasons to go there, so any dream of a trip always got shoved to the bottom of my list. Like seeing Mt. Rushmore, Pearl Harbor, Normandy Beach and the U.S. Open, it was unquestionably on my mental list of things to see and do before I die. There would be plenty of time after the kids were grown and gone and money wasn't so scarce to start checking off my list. Or, would there be? With our beach chairs arranged in a semi-circle so we could gaze out at the ocean and the horizon beyond, we embarked on a heart-to-heart discussion about all the things we wanted to see and do before we were too old and decrepit to enjoy them. We came up with a simply marvelous plan.

Suddenly chilled by a breathtaking sunset, but finally in control of our paranoia, we started gathering up all of our belongings and headed back to the condo. In the fading light, we spotted a lone surf fisherman and an egret poised on one leg. The fisherman, intent on his catch, ignored us, but the bird cocked its head and eyed us curiously. We were all that was left of the summer parade. A few minutes before, we made a pact that the next September, all four of us would take another road trip a little further north that would definitely include tennis. We didn't know how we'd pull it off or where the extra money would come from, but as Scarlett O'Hara would do, we'd think about that another day.

Spontaneously, we cranked up an unrehearsed but riveting rendition of "New York, New York."

"Start spreading the news, we're leaving today. We want to be a part of it-New York, New York. These little town blues are melting away, We're gonna make a brand new start of it -in old New York." Those were the only words of the song we could recall, so we commenced to improvising the chorus with, "Bomp, bomp, datta, datta, bomp, bomp, datta, datta-a-a," Liza Minnelli style, kicking up the sand, using our beach towels as makeshift boas, until we fell down into the sugar-white sand and laughed until we cried.

Once again, the V.G. s had managed to rip victory from the jaws of defeat.

Karen C. Rasberry

The Long, Long Chapter Without a Name...

The night that I sat down at my computer and pecked out the first sentence that would eventually evolve into this book, I had just paid my first installment towards our trip to New York City. My plan was, if I ever got that far along, to tell the story of our trip and a tennis player's dream come true of going to the U.S. Open as the closing chapter. The trouble is that one chapter couldn't possibly capture all that there is to say about such a life-altering, mind-boggling journey.

My first task was to think of a catchy title that would tempt the reader to flip to the end instead of starting with the first page. The distressing predicament was that there were so many titles that came to mind, it was impossible to choose just one. As a result, this chapter has been proclaimed "The Long, Long Chapter Without a Name." Even with no name, I think it has still come off as quite catchy.

After an outwardly nauseating journey which included cars, tiny little planes, great big planes chock full of aspiring terrorists, airport escalators, limousines, ferry boats, throbbing feet, taxis, that foul-smelling Hell hole called the subway (my personal favorite), and toward the end, a severe yearning for a motorized wheelchair, it was originally going to be named "Pass the Dramamine and the Lysol Please."

Upon our return, after I had recovered a bit from the trauma of visiting a city inhabited by eight million zillion people (444 times larger than the town where I come from and four times more populous than the entire state of Mississippi), there was no doubt in my mind that it would be titled "The Big Apple Took a Bite Out of Me."

Nobody has asked me, but I believe that New Yorkers need to slow it down a notch or two. They all seem as if they are too "important" and busy for their own good. The trouble with their slowing down is that they don't have any front porches to sit on. I bet you that not a handful of those Wall Street wonders ever sat on a front porch with his grandmother and shelled a bushel of peas. How many of them ever walked barefoot two miles down a dusty gravel road just so they could get a banana Popsicle and a Moon Pie at the country store? If they ever sat on an ice cream freezer while their daddy labored with the last few turns of the handle or went to the watermelon patch with their grandpa to thump around for the perfect melon, they would know how to slow it down a notch or two. The poor souls just don't know what they are missing. Bless their Dow Jones industrialized hearts. They assume they are living the good life amidst all that concrete, steel, and masses of humanity. It disturbs me that they believe we Southerners speak slowly and move about more leisurely because we are intellectually and culturally deprived. In reality, we are that way because we wouldn't have it any other way. They all may be in a hurry because they want to be. Considering how short life is, they'll never convince me that they are living life the way it ought to be lived.

A country girl like me, who was lulled to sleep at night by the lonesome songs of whippoorwills rather than emergency sirens, who woke up to hot grits swimming in butter instead of cold, rubbery bagels for breakfast, dined on fried catfish, hushpuppies and coleslaw rather than sushi for supper, would prefer to say "ya'll" instead of "you guys" and comes from a village whose highest building is only four stories tall, can't visit a place like NYC and return home completely intact. The magnitude of it all was, to say the least, overwhelming. You can take the girl out of the country, but you can't take the country out of the girl— without a fight.

Two weeks into September, when my supposed car, air, sea, and subway sickness had not subsided, and an emergency cholecystectomy was performed, it was going to be called "I Almost Left My Gallbladder in NYC" as a parody of the song "I Left My Heart in San Francisco." Gallbladders and the appendix are exactly the same. We don't really pay them that much mind since we can live without either or both of them. But, you let one of them flare up and you will do anything, and I do mean ANYTHING, to get rid of it. If my trip to NYC had been just a few days later, I would have had no choice but to leave my gallbladder, which my surgeon described as a little sack of marbles, in New York City with eight million strangers who didn't know me or it from Adam's house cat.

After my out-of-this-world laparoscopic procedure, while convalescing and devouring every word of the latest Tennis magazine as it recapped the highlights of an all-American final at the U.S. Open, I decided that it duly must be called "Looking for Pete." Affirmative. It would be titled "Looking for Pete," not just because he defeated Andre in four punishing sets, but on the premise that if our dear, fellow sojourner and beloved V.G. had said "I wanna see Pete" one more time, we were going to strangle her with a blow dryer cord and throw her into the Hudson River. We all love Pete as much as the next libidinous, tennis-playing, American woman, but her fixation with him had reached a fever pitch. We were alarmed that she was going to do something crazy that would plaster our faces on the cover of the National Enquirer or on the opening news segment of the Today Show.

Ann Curry would inform Today Show viewers in a somber voice, "Last night at Flushing Meadows, home of the U.S. Open, Pete Sampras was attacked by a female admirer as he made his way from Arthur Ashe Stadium after winning his match with Greg Rusedski. As the woman was apprehended by police, she repeatedly screamed, "You don't understand. I would never hurt him! All I wanted to do was touch his tennis balls and that curly, black hair." It is not known if there were any others involved in the attack, but three females, thought to be traveling companions of the attacker, were questioned and released after denying that they had ever met the deranged woman."

So far this chapter does makes our trip to New York sound as if it were more of a fiasco than a dream come true. Do not be misled. It was much more than a dream come true, and we've got 619 pictures to prove it. The only V.G. who had previously been to NYC, brought her digital camera and served as the official photographer and goodwill ambassador from Mississippi. She captured every single moment, except for when we went to the bathroom, which was more than plenty for two of us and not enough for the other two. Put four immodest women whose bodily functions have gotten all out of sync, one of them whose gallbladder is just before erupting, in one hotel room with just one bathroom, and you've got yourself an Emmy winning, primetime sitcom/drama. Imagine the Golden Girls meet Friends on E.R.

Our ambassador missed talking to only a dozen or less of the eight million residents of that fair city. She is truly amazing when she puts her mind to something. It's unbelievable that she is a CPA. Accountants are supposed to be nerdy, introverted, and boring, not charming men magnets with a gift of gab, who always seem to find themselves in the spotlight. In tribute to her, this chapter was almost named "Our Fifteen Minutes of Fame" because her charm and shameless flirting with a Today Show cameraman got us on national television for two whole minutes.

The enraptured cameraman intentionally positioned Katie Couric and Ann Curry in such a way that we were all on camera smiling and waving to the folks back home as they chit chatted about something or another that all the viewers couldn't possibly have paid any attention to because they were so distracted by the frenzied women in the background. The chances of making our debut on national television were also highly improved by the fact that we were in possession of a tennis ball the size of Uranus.

One of the V.G. s has the admirable virtue of being a thoughtful and generous individual, with a pocketbook as big as her heart to fund her philanthropic efforts. She felt the need to purchase a souvenir for every blood relative, in-law, out-law, and acquaintance back in lil' ole' Mississippi. She had herself a gratifying time picking out the perfect gift for each and every one, never taking into account how she would get said gifts back to Mississippi when her luggage already exceeded what was necessary to take a trip around the globe. Among the gifts, was a gargantuan tennis ball she purchased at the U.S. Open for her little nephew, because every three year old wants and needs a tennis ball the size of a planet.

Amazingly, on the morning of our departure, she did find a place for all of her gifts. It took three of us standing on her suitcases, with the bellhop and a Sumo wrestler whom we recruited from the room next door, tugging on the zippers, but we got those suckers closed up tighter than Dick's hat band. God be with any person standing near them if the zippers broke. Then we looked around the room to see if anything had been omitted. "Ohhh, craaap!!," we moaned as a quartet. The monolithic tennis ball sat on the bed glaring at us as luminously as the sun.

"Just leave it here," someone sternly suggested. "No way! I paid forty dollars for the blasted thing. We will just have to take turns carrying it, because that baby already knows I bought him a gift." Being the sympathetic aunties that we are, we took turns lugging it southward through LaGuardia, Hartsfield in Atlanta, on down to New Orleans, then back up to Laurel, Mississippi. We blasphemed it on three different airplanes and reviled it for a thousand miles as we alternately ate, slept, and used the restroom with it upon our laps. By jiminy, little Nicholas got his tennis ball, and all was right with the world.

Back to the Today Show. We always thought so before we saw her in person, but that Katie Couric is absolutely cuter than a speckled puppy under a red wagon. She was wearing a pinkish boucle' business suit and wasn't even wearing panty hose. Her shapely, svelte legs didn't have a single dimple, spider vein, freckle, or cell of fat on them. We all just hated her guts for being so perky and perfect at that time of the morning. We were carrying bags and black circles under our eyes and looked like raccoons on steroids, but not Katie. She was fresh as a daffodil, and her under the eye area gave nary a clue that she rolled out of bed at 3:00 A.M.

Big Al Roker was the most jovial fellow you would ever want to meet, and his skin was a smooth milk chocolate color that made you want to smack his cheeks to see if they tasted like a Hershey's kiss. Ann Curry wasn't as big as a toot and had creamy flawless skin and coal black hair. She'd be gorgeous with no makeup, but they had done her up so that she all but glowed in the early morning light. It ought to be against the law to look that good at such a ridiculously early hour of the day. All of them had an aura about them that we average folk just don't have. I believe it is called "star quality." It's tragically unfair that some people turned out to be so perfect, and the rest of us have to go through life carrying a croaker sack full of makeup just so we will not be offensive to the naked eye.

Mesmerizing a cameraman at 6:30 in the morning was remarkable, considering we weren't much to look at after running on eight hours of sleep in five days; but what Miss Congeniality did the night before at the Open was a doozey. You may or may not know, but the 2002 U.S. Open went down in the books as one of the soggiest in history. We lucked up on Saturday and enjoyed some unbelievably inspiring tennis all day without any rain. We also had tickets for Monday's day session, but the rain kept coming down sideways and in sheets and buckets all day long. In the South we call them "gully washers" or "frog stranglers." I don't know what they call it in New York City, but as my grandpa liked to say, it "rained like a cow pissin' on a flat rock" for two days and three nights.

Since I was plumb worn out from shopping while trying to avoid poking the eyes out of at least four million people with my "toodolla," Chinatown umbrella, and feeling a tad bilious to boot, I opted not to go with them to Flushing Meadows after the rain moved out. As for that umbrella, you absolutely get what you pay for. The first time the wind whipped up, that flimsy $2.00 umbrella promptly turned itself inside out and stayed that way all day long. It was collecting rain like a birdbath instead of repelling it. I finally got fed up with it and threw the piece of junk at, not into, a garbage can outside of Macy's.

"Ya'll have lost your minds. It's going to start raining again just like it did last night. If you can even get a ticket, it will be up in the airspace of LaGuardia Airport. You go right on ahead. I'm going to stay right here, eat a roll of Tums, take a Dramamine and watch it all on T.V."

Lo and behold, I awoke from a little catnap and groggily turned my eyes to the television. Was I dreaming? My mind couldn't register what I was seeing! The man magnet had done it again. As the camera panned the stadium, there they were, the V.G. s, sitting fourth row, mid-court within spitting distance of Andy Roddick, Pete Sampras, and Andre Agassi. I was going to be force fed crow for the rest of my life. At 2:00 A.M., they burst into the room, pounced on top of me, and proceeded to tell me all about what I had missed.

"No, I didn't miss a thing. I saw it all, even you three sirens laughing, talking, gawking and flirting right there in living color on the U.S.A. channel."

"Tell me, how did you get those seats? No! No! I'll tell you. Miss Prissy Pants Motor Mouth sweet-talked a security guard into letting her come down out of the nosebleed section to take a picture of Andy. In the 15 seconds it took to snap a picture, she struck up a conversation with a gentleman who, no doubt, had enough money to burn a wet mule, or he had connections with Steven Spielberg or some unbelievable story like that. He just so happened to have three extra seats that you three harlots gladly helped him fill. He was completely blown away by your Southern accents and enticed you to accompany him to his hotel for cocktails when the match was over. Of course, you declined his indecent proposal. Am I right?"

"Sugar britches" burst into giggles and said, "Yep, that's just about how it went, except he was a good friend of Jack Nicholson, and he didn't ask us up to his hotel room. It was a penthouse overlooking Central Park, and no, we didn't go."

This chapter also makes it appear that the four of us ventured off to New York blindly without any guidance or the companionship of other people. If that were the case, we would have never made it back to Mississippi. We'd still be underground in the subway labyrinth blindly searching for the yellow train to mid-town Manhattan and tap dancing for quarters to help finance our way back home. The nightmares are less frequent now that it's been a few months, but the subway was so traumatic for me that I have considered going into therapy.

We may be crazy, but we aren't insane. Of course we were not alone. We traipsed off to New York with eighteen other people, (six V.G. s in all, but two of them had their husbands to fret with) some other local tennis players, a couple of professional shoppers, and a few non-tennis players who just wanted to see the Statue of Liberty. You might find this odd, but the ringleader and organizer of our foray was none other than a Southern Baptist preacher with a penchant for tennis and the bright lights of New York City. He's been taking groups to the U.S. Open for umpteen years now and knows the city like he knows the book of Ecclesiastes.

Since we were so far from home, just knowing that we had a man-of-the-cloth in our midst made us feel more at peace with the fact that we could die at any second, especially when the pilots cranked up that jet in New Orleans. Don't you just love the adrenaline rush you get when the flight attendants demonstrate the obligatory "what to do in the unlikely event of a sudden loss in cabin pressure" procedure? And what about the peace of mind you get just knowing that you can use your seat cushion as a flotation device? Other than the Mississippi River, after you take off in New Orleans, the flight path to New York doesn't necessarily include any bodies of water large enough to accommodate a huge jetliner, which renders a flotation device about as useful as a screen door on a submarine. In the unhappy event of loss of cabin pressure, the flight attendants should tell the truth and instruct you to, "Put your head between your knees and kiss your sweet ass goodbye, because it's history." Do not be dismayed. You can take comfort in all the news headlines it will make when you go down in a blaze of glory into farmer McDonald's catfish pond in rural Georgia.

All the news networks could broadcast Mr. Jarvis McDonald in fine redneck form to the entire world, "Hit wuz awful, jus awful. Me and my ole' lady wuz sittin' on the porch waitin' fer the mail to run. That's when we heered it. Sounded jus like a big jut was fixin' to land ona house. Well, hit wuz a big jut areplane, 'cept hit crashed nose first into my catfish pon. Hit sounded like the end of the worl. Them pore folks didn't know what happent. Hit kilt ever las one of my catfish an all em people too. You won't never catch me on one a them thar planes. I betche hit wuz zem terrist agin."

This is not too terribly off the subject, so would you please ponder this? Does disaster, especially in the South, exclusively strike unsightly people who have no working knowledge of the English language, or do the news networks bring a busload of unkempt, illiterate, professional disaster victims to interview so they won't have to bother the real victims? Anyone can understand looking a bit disheveled, considering you just went for a ride on a tornado in your mobile home, but please don't get on T.V. with a moment-by-terrifying-moment account of it if you didn't finish the sixth grade.

For many of us, it was the first time we had flown since September 11. We felt that perchance some angels would be flying alongside us and would keep the wings from falling off if our numbers happened to pop up. The angels would sweetly plead, "No, not this plane, Lord. There's a Baptist preacher and a whole bunch of good folks on board who wanted to attend the U.S. Open before they died. Father, except for the preacher, who

112

has been heard to say "shucks" very loudly, they swear a little on the tennis court and some of them have been known to forget how to act in public, but You know they do try their best to be good. If we could make a suggestion Lord, Osama Bin Laden and Al-Qaeda are still out there somewhere planning another attack. Possibly, if it is in Your will, You could spare these kind people and take him and those infidels instead."

In the unlikely event that the angels weren't flying with us and terrorists abruptly commandeered the plane, we were confident that the preacher could persuade them to convert to Christianity, which would squelch all their desires to crash planes into buildings. If that failed, we knew that he, with a little help from the other tennis boys, was big enough, tough enough, and brave enough to take out the meanest terrorist alive. Either way, we were in good hands. For these reasons, this chapter also could have been titled, "In Good Hands With the Preacher Man."

Walking into the United States Tennis Center at Flushing Meadows on that late August morning was a defining moment that will forever be etched in my memory. It ranks right up there with getting my first brassiere, finally passing my driver's license exam, seeing Elvis, and holding Conway Twitty's hand as he growled, "I'd love to lay you down." August 31, 2002, set an all-time record for the U.S. Open with 55,734 fans in attendance. Although the V.G. s had more than enough company, it was our day and our dream that was coming true.

We had mentally planned, re-planned, talked about who we wanted to see play, packed, and re-packed for six whole months. Would it still be warm in New York in September, or do you think it might turn cool or, Heaven forbid, rain? Crap. It could even snow. We packed everything from tank tops to thermal underwear, but at least we were prepared. My son was getting married the week before our departure. I barely had enough sense to recite my name, much less think about what clothes to take to New York City, and the V.G. s were calling me every hour on the hour to ask my opinion.

There were moments of sheer terror, but the wedding went off without a hitch—no hysterical weeping from the mother of the groom, no fainting and no objections from the crowd. Our plane didn't crash into a catfish pond, and our luggage, which weighed no less than 350 pounds apiece, was actually going round and round on the carousel when we went to claim it. I guarantee you that N.A.S.A. sends astronauts into space with less preparation. When that airplane finally touched down, we were jet-lagged, ill as snakes and in desperate need of some shut-eye. At last, after six full months of childlike anticipation, we had landed in the city of our dreams.

Not even we ever dreamed that the very first tennis professional we would lay our eyes on would be Monica Seles (number 6 in the world) in Arthur Ashe stadium. That was a pretty good start for a team of dreamers. Later, when we found ourselves back in Arthur Ashe stadium pulling for American James Blake (number 29) as he went down in five sets against the number one ranked player in the whole wide world, Lleyton Hewitt, it was a dream that we never wanted to awaken from.

We marveled a few minutes at Venus Williams (number 2) as she outclassed Martina Muller of Germany. We quickly established the fact that we didn't want to find ourselves across the net from the likes of her. What's more, the four of us put together couldn't take her to deuce. The match would be over before it started. Serena saw no action that day, but we did get to stargaze as she pulled for her big sister, probably sensing she would meet her in the finals **again.** Then it was Kim Clijsters, number seven in the world, as she defeated an opponent with a name I can neither spell or pronounce. World-class tennis was happening on all the outer courts as well. We hopped from court to court and worried about what we were missing on the court next door.

The practice courts drew nearly as much attention as the match courts. We saw Hingis, Alexandra Stevenson, and Roddick leisurely hitting a few warm up balls with their coaches. It was rumored that Kournikova was on her way to warm up, but we didn't even get a glimpse of her. The first thing everyone asked when I got home was, "Did you see the little hottie, Kournikova?" I lied. "Oh yeah. But, she's not really as gorgeous in person as she is on television, and she's only ranked number 34 in the world. She's not that big of a deal to me." The truth is that she is so absolutely perfect that she makes me want to hang myself with racquet string.

It was on court seven that we fell into complete lust with two players from France. We weren't sure if it was Michael Llodra or

Fabrice Santoro, but one of them had the most perfect legs we had ever seen on a male specimen. Our Chippendales fell victim to Knowles and Nestor in straight sets, but just seeing those legs made every dime we spent getting to the U.S. Open worth it.

Later in the day, court seven had again drawn quite a crowd, so we hurried over to see who was playing. Judging from the mass of people, it had to be somebody great. It was none other than Martina Navratilova playing a women's doubles match. I couldn't miss the opportunity to see an icon of women's tennis, but the crowd was much too deep, and I was way too short to see. So, I shimmied up a planter onto a garbage can where I watched in awe until a security officer threatened to arrest me if I didn't come down immediately. Just as well. A light mist had begun to fall, so I went to find the other V.G. s My one day at the Open was swiftly coming to a close. An old familiar feeling of dread was creeping in.

Do you remember when you were a kid and doing something that was so much fun that you just couldn't bear to stop doing it? Like playing in the yard past dark in the summer, catching lightnin' bugs in a Mason jar, or swimming in a frigid, spring-fed lake until you turned purple or eating popcorn at a matinee, praying that the movie would never end and that you could kiss Elvis like Ann-Margret did. I have shared all this so you can understand what it felt like when we left the U.S. Open that afternoon. As we waited for the subway train that would take us back to our hotel, it felt exactly like being forced to come inside or get out of the water or realizing that the movie would end and that you would never get to kiss Elvis.

Well, here we are at the end of "The Long, Long Chapter Without a Name." Don't breathe a sigh of relief yet, because it's not exactly the end. This chapter and probably a third of this book was written to delay writing these next few paragraphs. This hasn't been formally taught to me as I am not formally educated in the art of writing, but the conclusion of any story or book, no matter how nonsensical it has been, should have some substance that gives the reader something to "chew on" when he has finished reading it. Here's my untrained attempt at substance.

Stepping into the bright lights of Times Square with throngs of people purposely dashing about in all directions gave me a sense of how infinite the world really is and how small and insignificant I really am. Watching professional tennis players, with all their quickness, power and athleticism, made we question why I even attempt to play the game.

Finally seeing the Statue of Liberty helped me capture the essence of my daddy in his youth during World War II. He told me only recently that he had spent several lonely months living in barracks on Pier 90 while commissioning a ship. While stationed in New York, he and a couple of other sailors "borrowed" a motorboat from the U.S. Navy, took a joy ride on the Hudson River to the base of "Miss Liberty," anchored and climbed to the top. He was only twenty-three or four years old at the time. Now, he's eighty-four.

Attending the fabulous Broadway production of The Lion King filled me with terrible guilt because my daughter had begged me to take her with me to New York. It was her 17th birthday and the first time that I was not there to celebrate one of the two best things that ever happened to me. She had watched the cartoon version thirty-seven times and could sing every ballad word-for-word in perfect pitch when she was still in bows and lace. Once upon a time she slept with Simba, Nala and Mufasa. Now, they sleep alone in her toy chest.

Seeing the famous skyline of New York City at night, with all its familiar landmarks, literally took my breath away. It was what was missing from the skyline in the broad daylight that shook me right down to my soul.

Hang in here with me because there is a moral to this story. On a drizzly Sunday morning on September 1, 2002, our entire entourage took a somber walk past Wall Street to view the haunting, cavernous scar where the Twin Towers still stood a year earlier. It was a tremendously spiritual moment for each of us in our own measure. If you call yourself a patriot and can go there without shedding a few tears or at least getting a knot in your throat, you need to find a new country to call home. Within a few moments, something came to me in a tearful revelation. We didn't go to New York solely to see the U.S. Open, the Statue of Liberty, the Empire State Building or the neon lights of Broadway. We went to New York searching for something that none of us will ever find—closure to a chapter of American history that shouldn't and couldn't have possibly happened.

Standing wordlessly, gazing through a cyclone fence at Ground Zero, all of my muddled emotions were about to became crystal clear. Stuck between the wires of the fence, was a letter left by a brokenhearted loved one. The ink had faded, but the message became indelibly printed on my heart. Through eyes brimming with tears I read: "It has been almost a year and my heart is still broken into tiny pieces that will never fit together again. The ones who took you from me have no hearts. They tried to take everything that is precious away from me, from you, from all of us. But, they will never take away my freedom, my memories, or my love. You have, I will, and our nation will rise above this hatred. We who have been left behind will soar with eagles while you soar with angels' wings. Until I see you again. Love forever and always, Amanda." There was no closure to be found, but in the immeasurable sorrow, I found inspiration.

Let's stop the tape and rewind for a few seconds. Never mind what I felt earlier in Times Square. It had become crystal clear that no matter how small and insignificant we might feel, everyone has a purpose for living.

U.S. Open class tennis players are the exception to the rule— indeed as rare as the Hope Diamond. It is we, the weekend, week-night, year-in and year-out, league-playing warriors that are the rule. I have decided that I can and will for as long as I am able, continue to play tennis with as much passion and heart as the top ranked tennis players in the world. Even if you are not the best at something, it's the camaraderie, the trying and the enjoyment you get out of it that counts.

Life is short but sweet for certain. If your dream is to conquer Mt. Everest, ride a camel across the Sahara Desert, or run a marathon; do it now, before it's too late. Time stands still for no man. Just in case you haven't noticed, the older you get, the faster the sand sifts through the hourglass. If my daddy could reclaim sixty years of his life and return to the war years, as horrific as they were, certainly he would. My daughter is perfectly happy being seventeen. I wish she were still seven, so we could cuddle on the couch to watch the Lion King one more time.

In the game of tennis, love doesn't mean a thing. In the circle of life, it means **everything**. If you love somebody, tell them so every single day. If you find that someone is unlovable, turn the other cheek and love the daylights out of everybody else.

Life has subtle, enduring ways of teaching us little lessons. Triumphs, as well as defeat, are meant to teach us determination and humility. We should revel in our victories, but only for a day. Triumph is, sooner or later, followed by defeat. You don't need to be reminded that not one soul currently walking around on this Earth comes remotely close to being perfect. Even the best players in the world, with all their accolades, have made more than a few unforced errors in the game and in life. Not if, but when, you make an unforced error, pick yourself up, put the puzzle back together, and keep striving until you get it right.

I'm just a tennis-playing nobody who had the dream to write a silly little book about recreational tennis players. More than once, I almost threw in the towel, stayed on the baseline and lost the match. Thanks to my girls, the one and only V.G. s, for supplying me with the motivation and encouragement to be more aggressive, get to the net, and "put the ball away."

Now, the ball is in your court. It's your serve, 1-love, first set. Absolutely anything could happen. That's what is so totally amazing about tennis, love, and life.

About the Author

Karen C. Rasberry has been a free-lance writer for the past five years. Her work has been published in Country, Country Extra, The Newsletter for Retired Veterans, and Today in Mississippi. She wrote as a guest columnist for the Laurel Leader-Call and was voted Best Columnist in 2000 by the readers in the circulation area of the newspaper. Much of her writing is nostalgic and evokes warmhearted memories of growing up in the South. The Volley Girls' Book of Life, Love, and Unforced Errors was inspired by her "addiction" to tennis and a group of eclectic women who share her passion for the game. When she is not playing tennis or writing, she works as a Realtor in Laurel, Mississippi.